GLASGOW'S EAST END

THROUGH TIME

Gordon Adams

AMBERLEY PUBLISHING

For Anna & Tommy O'Connor

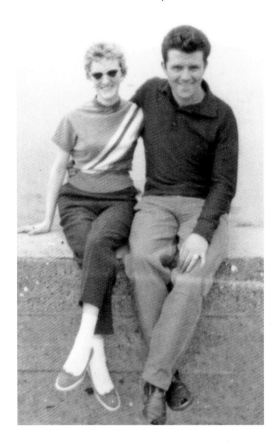

First published 2014

Amberley Publishing
The Hill, Stroud
Gloucestershire, GL5 4EP

www.amberley-books.com

Copyright © Gordon Adams, 2014

The right of Gordon Adams to be identified as the
Author of this work has been asserted in
accordance with the Copyrights, Designs and
Patents Act 1988.

ISBN 978 1 4456 3850 8 (print)
ISBN 978 1 4456 3854 6 (ebook)

British Library Cataloguing in Publication Data.
A catalogue record for this book is available from
the British Library.

Typesetting by Amberley Publishing.
Printed in the UK.

Acknowledgements

I should like to thank everyone who has contributed to the production of this book, particularly Gary O'Connor for his unfailing support while living through chaos and for the invaluable proof-reading which he undertook, and the staff at Amberley for their patience. Special thanks to Glasgow Libraries and Glasgow Life for photo opportunities and permission to reproduce various images. Thanks also to Jim Clark at Clyde Gateway & Gerry Blaikie.

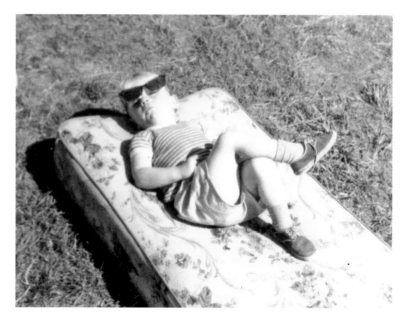

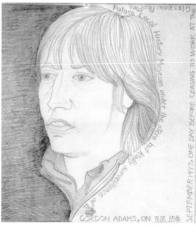

The author in 1977 after a brief soujourn at the People's Palace Museum, by the artist in residence Alasdair Gray.

Introduction

As a native of Bridgeton, I first noticed, in 1974, that there seemed to be an increasing number of demolitions taking place within the familiar landscape of my childhood. My response at the time was to take some slides of Bridgeton, Calton, Mile End and Dalmarnock – the areas that seemed to be most affected – to preserve my memory of them. This sparked an abiding interest in the history of those areas, which later extended to Tollcross, where had I moved some years earlier to a new Corporation house, and eventually to all of the districts of the East End of the city. I feel really fortunate to have recorded so much at the time because now there is very little left of the areas I knew to remind me of my earliest home.

The biggest impact in my own recollection was the seemingly massive slum clearances of the early period of the Glasgow Eastern Area Renewal (GEAR) project, which started around 1976. I remember well the great swathes of derelict land that opened up with the removal of large numbers of tenements, factories, churches, shops and all the other buildings that inhabited my world. They were eventually replaced by modern housing estates, many even with gardens, and a wild intrusion of greenery claiming places where it had not existed for the best part of 100 years. I don't recall the upsurge in employment that GEAR had hoped for, and there certainly seemed to be fewer factories or shops in the area offering work. The new streets looked rather naked in comparison to the old, for the greater part of the population had been moved elsewhere while the well-intentioned destruction took place. The sense of community also seemed to have been lost, and I am honestly not sure if it has ever been found again.

The other major and most recent change to my own East End has been the advent of Clyde Gateway, which has been involved in many major and minor projects throughout the area, like the restoration of the Olympia at Bridgeton Cross – particularly in the run up to the Commonwealth Games. It must be forgiven for actually crossing the river and extending its efforts into Rutherglen!

Having explained my motivation for undertaking this book, I must now say why I have done so in my own particular fashion, since not all East End aficionados may not consider the book as much of a success as I do. I admit from the start that I have almost entirely included only the inner-city areas. This is partly because of limited space, but also because I have always distinguished between the East End of Glasgow and East Glasgow. I consider the latter to contain the housing schemes built since the turn of the twentieth century to the present time that East-Enders moved out to. In addition are those small but independent outlying districts, which were not exactly dragged kicking and screaming into the city precincts, but some inhabitants of which still consider themselves as being from places like Baillieston and not Glasgow.

This book has also allowed me the opportunity to share some of the photographs I have taken over a very long time, and which might otherwise be lost to posterity. I have not always opted for the most iconic, which tend to be reproduced *ad infinitum*. Some might be considered quite quirky – not necessarily a bad thing in a recounting of history.

When trying to recreate some of the modern scenes for comparison with the older ones, which is the basic theme of this volume, it rapidly became apparent how many old street scenes were taken from the upstairs of trams. Some others were obviously taken by the photographer standing in the middle of a road. As traffic was fairly minimal in the earliest days, this had presented no difficulty, whereas now it involves taking your life in your hands to reproduce the scenes. Other early photographs have been taken from the top of high rise flats that no longer exist or other high places that are no longer accessible. One surprising factor, especially within the East End, is the number of trees, where before there were none. Beautiful as this is, it has the drawback of hindering comparative views, so some updates had to take this into account. It is also hugely difficult not to include images of yet more new houses as they roll over fields, old industrial sites and various other nooks and crannies. Eventually, one housing estate begins to look exactly like another. Where necessary, I have chosen to exercise my author's prerogative of doing what I think best in the circumstances. I think this enhances rather than hinders the process.

I do hope that you will enjoy this book – I won't say 'as much as I have enjoyed producing it' because the act of creation is not always an easy one. Enjoy the idiosyncrasies that creep in here and there, and I hope that at least some of these images evoke pleasant memories for you.

Gordon Adams

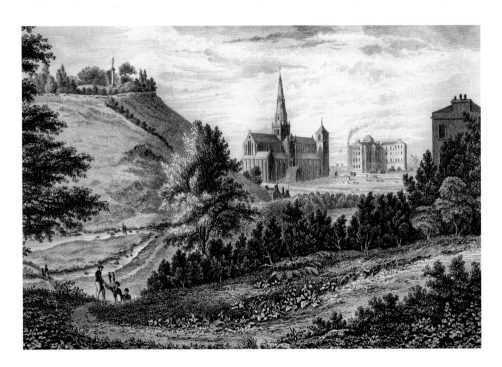

Glasgow Cathedral

A view on the banks of the Molendinar Burn in 1828, from the north. To the left is the drumlin of the Fir Park, with its 1825 monument to the Protestant reformer John Knox. This was transformed into the Necropolis in 1833. To the right is the main block of the original Royal Infirmary. The once pristine Molendinar Burn, in the valley, was culverted over in 1878 as a health hazard, and Wishart Street laid down over it. By 2014, the Royal Infirmary has been greatly extended to engulf all available grounds to the north.

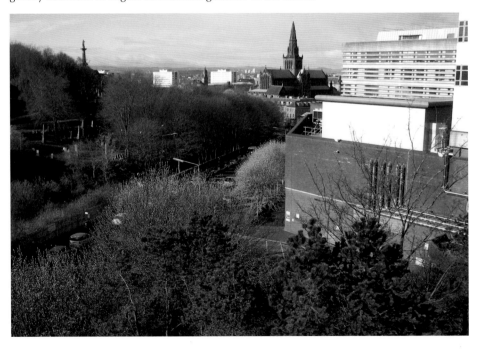

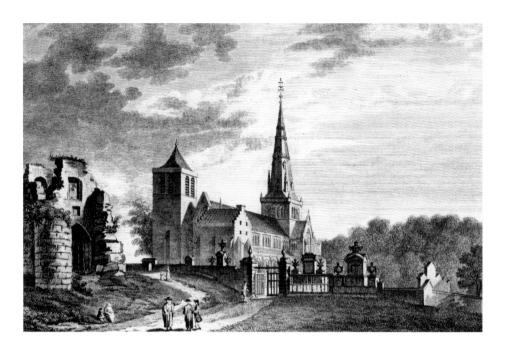

Glasgow Cathedral

Dating from the twelfth century, but built on the site of earlier structures. This 1780 view from the south-west includes the two towers that were removed in 1846–48 during restoration work, in the mistaken belief that they were only recent additions. To the left are the ruins of the Bishop's Castle, which were soon to be removed to make way for the construction of the Royal Infirmary in 1794. Time and industrial pollution have inevitably taken their toll on the cathedral. Here, in 2014, the most recent restoration work was being concluded.

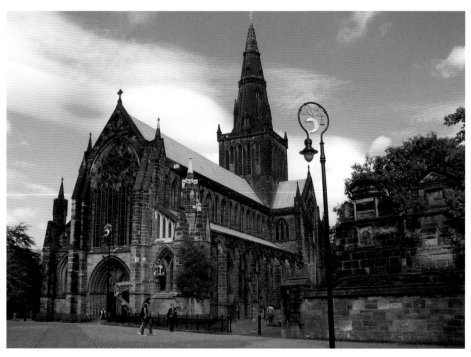

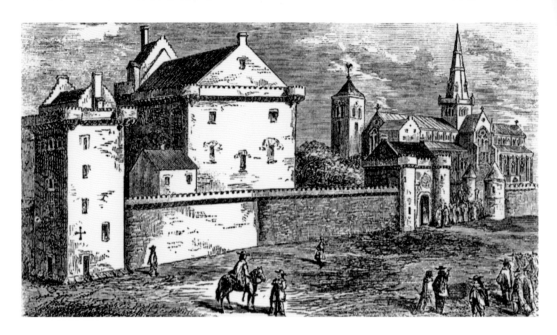

Bishop's Castle

The bishop's castle was situated to the west of his cathedral and dates from at least 1258. Fortification of the bishop's residence was essential given the temporal authority that was exercised by the Glasgow prelate during the turbulent history of medieval Scotland. On one occasion it was occupied by the troops of Edward I while Bishop Wishart was fighting in the War of Independence. The castle ruins were removed in 1789–92, and part of the site is now occupied by the St Mungo Museum of Religious Life and Art, built in a style that reflects the history of the location.

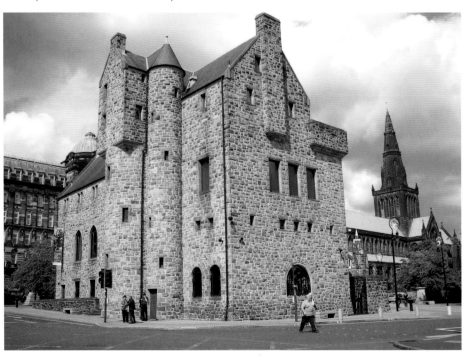

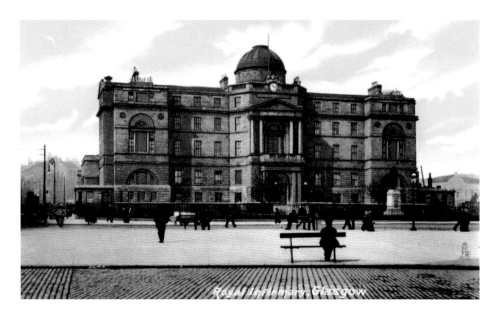

The Royal

For 220 years, the people of the East End have benefited from the services provided by 'the Royal'. In the eighteenth century, medical services for the poor were extremely limited. As a voluntary hospital, the Royal Infirmary went some way to addressing this. However, within 100 years, the hospital had already become too small to meet the demands of an increasing population. There followed a period of replacement and expansion that still continues today. The Queen Victoria Jubilee building, now fronting onto the Cathedral Precinct, replaced the original Adam Building. Although criticised as overwhelming the cathedral, it served a much needed and practical role.

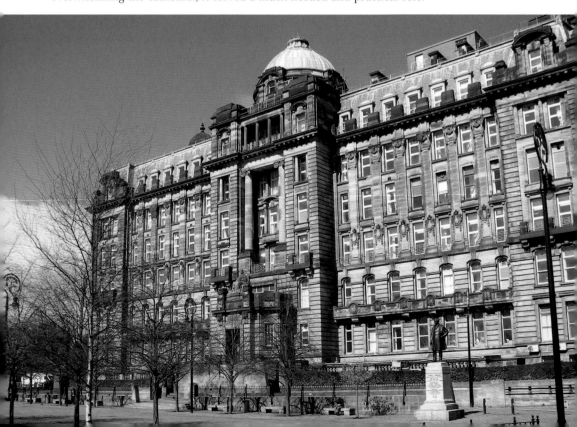

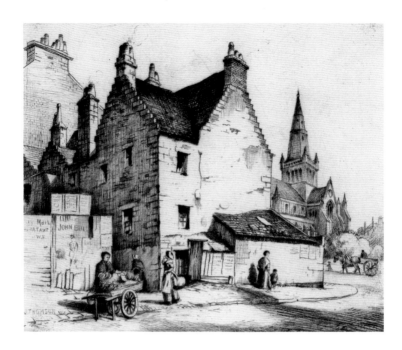

Provand's Lordship

This is the only medieval dwelling to survive the city centre's slum clearances. Built by the church in 1471 as part of St Nicholas's Hospital, it was later allocated to the Prebendary of Barlanark (or Provand). Prebends were lands of the parish that were allocated to Prebendaries (senior churchmen), to provide them with an income. Provand was a corruption of Prebend. The building served a variety of purposes in the following centuries and is now a museum. Miraculously, not only has the Prebendary's city house survived, but so has his country house at Provan Hall in Easterhouse.

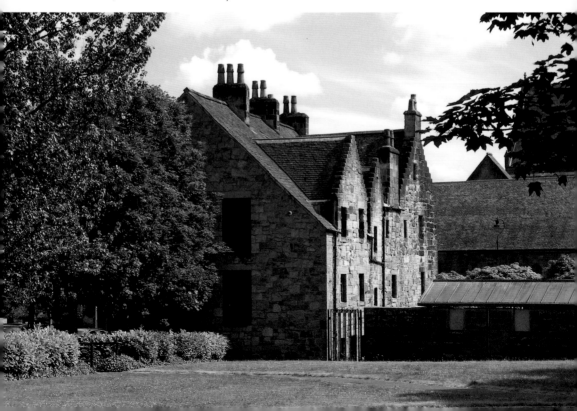

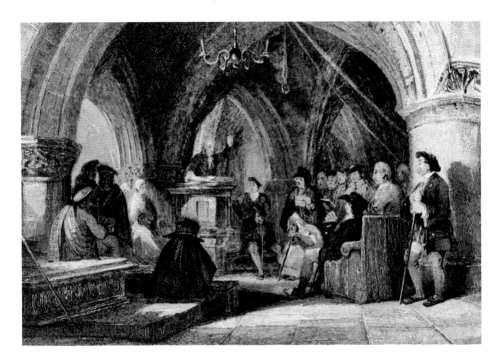

The Crypt of the Cathedral

Home to the Barony Parish congregation for 203 years. The Barony was established in *c.* 1595, but the congregation did not move from the crypt until 1799. It transferred to a new building on Cathedral Square, but the congregation outgrew this after only ninety years. An impressive red sandstone church on Castle Street replaced the old building in 1889, but the parish was ultimately terminated in 1985 after almost 400 years. Its church was acquired by Strathclyde University as a ceremonial space. A small chapel in the crypt of the cathedral, from whence it came, commemorates the Barony.

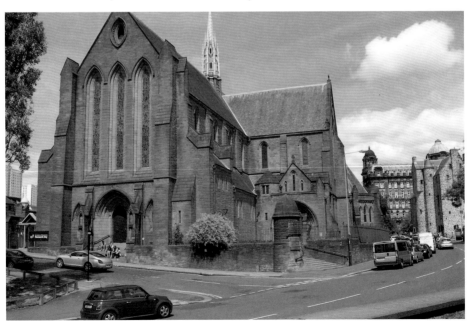

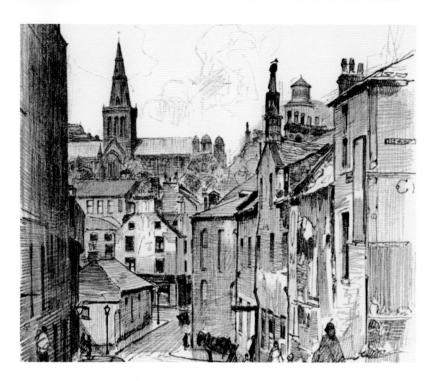

A 1926 Sketch by Robert Eadie

The winding passage beside the Moledinar Burn that became Ladywell Street. A remnant of a medieval street survives as a cul-de-sac leading off Wishart Street and terminates at Tennent's Wellpark Brewery, which has entirely submerged the rest. The ancient route had allowed approach to the cathedral from the south east and took its name from the well situated in the locale – the Lady Well – which provided a fresh water supply for local inhabitants. The well was closed around 1820 but the site is marked by an urn within a niche in the Necropolis boundary wall.

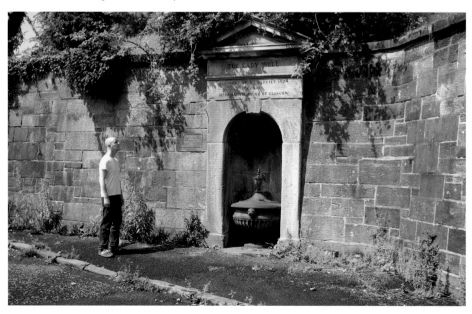

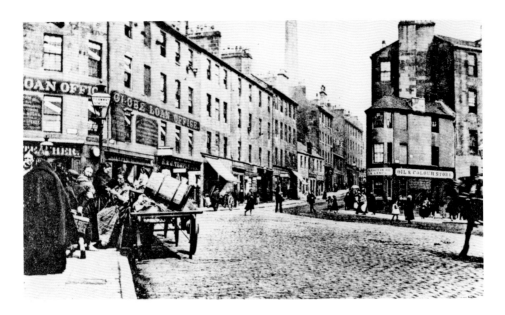

Bell o' the Brae

Where High Street runs uphill from its junction with George Street and Duke Street. All of the earlier buildings at this junction were demolished by the City Improvement Trust, and replaced by the highly ornate red sandstone tenements built from 1899–1902, creating an impressive entry to the upper High Street and the cathedral. The opportunity was also taken to reduce what had been a significant incline. This location is celebrated for an alleged military engagement in 1297 won by William Wallace against English troops from the garrison in the Bishop's Castle during the War of Independence.

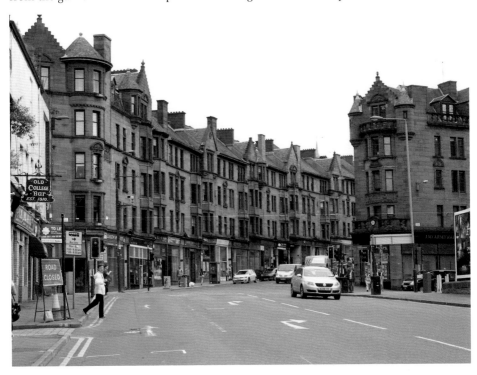

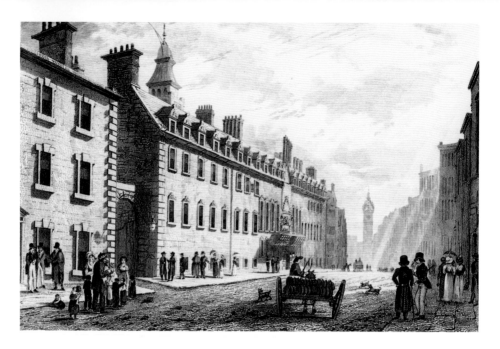

Glasgow University Fronting on to the High Street *c.* 1820

Founded in 1451, the university established a presence in High Street from 1453. A building programme in the mid-seventeenth century saw the removal of the decaying medieval structures that the college had acquired, and an extensive new complex was established. The whole site was eventually sold to the City of Glasgow Union Railway when the university migrated to the west end of the city in 1870 to escape the encroaching squalor, disease and debauchery of the High Street area. The ornate frontage was ultimately replaced by the functional but nondescript High Street railway station.

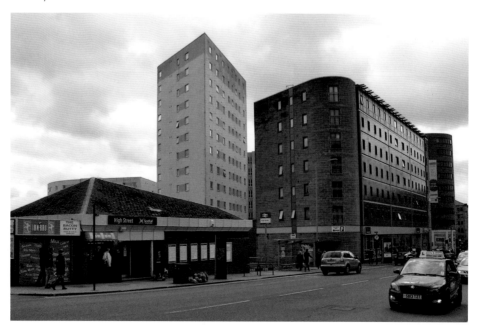

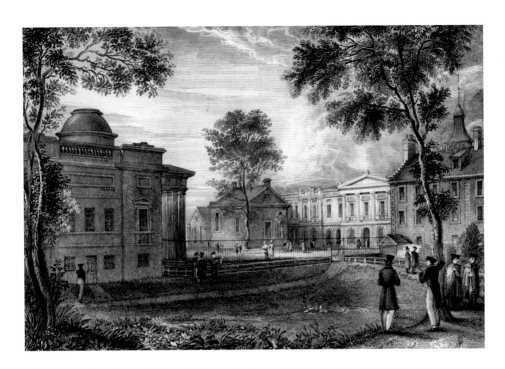

Glasgow University Had Owned Extensive Property West of the High Street

In this 1828 engraving, the first Hunterian Museum, built in 1804, can be seen to the left. The college library and then the Common Hall are to the right of this. The loss of such significant architecture to the city is tragic. The whole property was demolished to allow the creation of a railway line and goods yard. The latter is now derelict, but the railway line, which runs through the old grounds, is still in operation, as seen in High Street station below.

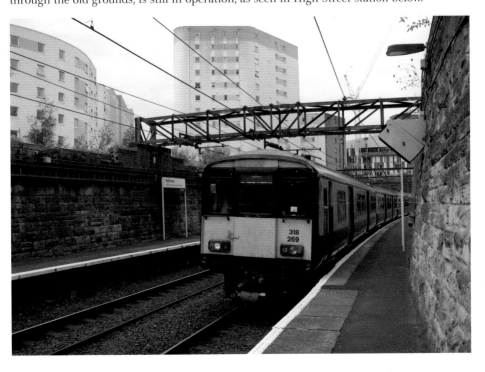

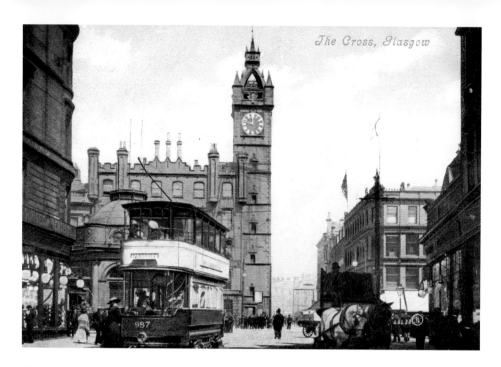

Glasgow Cross Looking Along the High Street *c.* 1906, with the Tolbooth and Steeple
Built in 1625–27 to replace earlier structures, the Tolbooth was where the town council met and courts were held. Eventually, space became inadequate and these responsibilities were transferred elsewhere. When the Cross was redesigned in 1921, the old building was demolished. The steeple was to be moved to create a new focal point, but this did not happen, and it remains where it has always stood, with traffic flowing awkwardly around it. The Mercat Cross was built in 1929, replacing a cross that stood there until 1659.

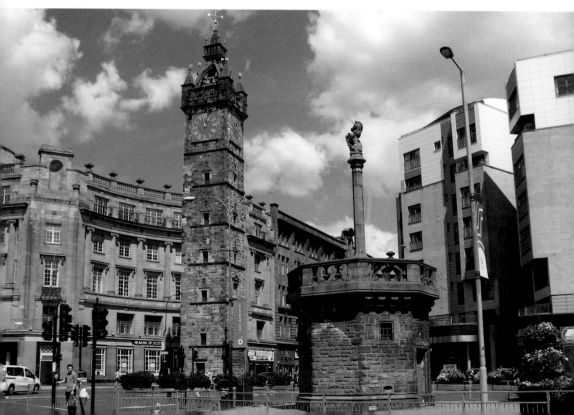

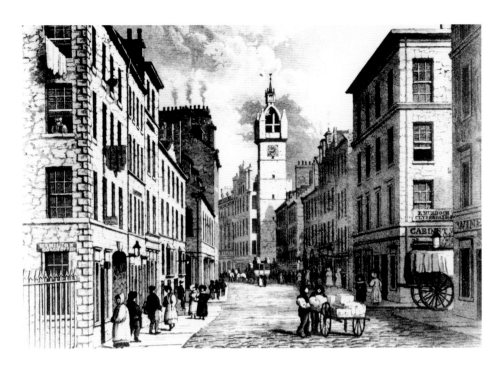

Glasgow Cross in 1832 from Gallowgate

One of the city's more ancient thoroughfares. Gallowgate runs from Glasgow Cross to Parkhead Cross, but the original only reached a short distance to the town's eastern limits, near present-day Great Dovehill Street, where the route was blocked by a town gate. Outside that barrier was a rough country road and the Gallowmuir, where executions took place. This may have given the route its name, but this remains just speculation. A disused railway bridge now obscures the view and most of the buildings shown have gone – victims of the railways or slum clearances.

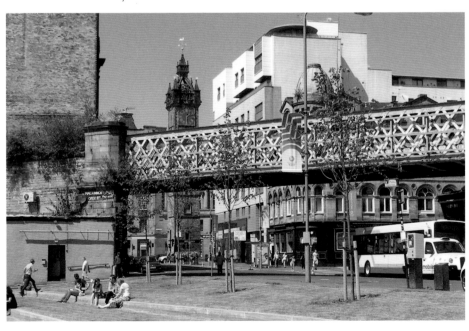

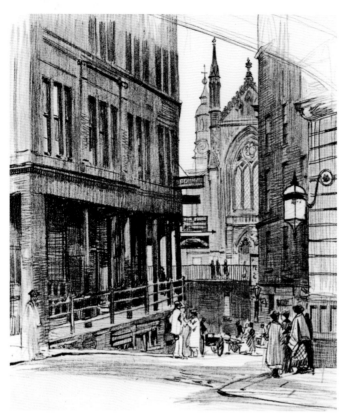

Shipka Pass, *c.* 1926

The source of the name of this old route leading off the Gallowgate towards St Andrew's Square is often speculated upon, but remains unresolved. Before demolition, some shops at the Pass displayed signs that read 'St Andrew's Pass's, which may denote local memory of the pass' original purpose of accessing the church. The route was probably bridged over when London Street – as it was called then – was driven through densely packed housing into the Saltmarket. The supports over the recently exposed underpass indicate its erection in 1826. The surrounding buildings were cleared in 2014 to create the adjacent park.

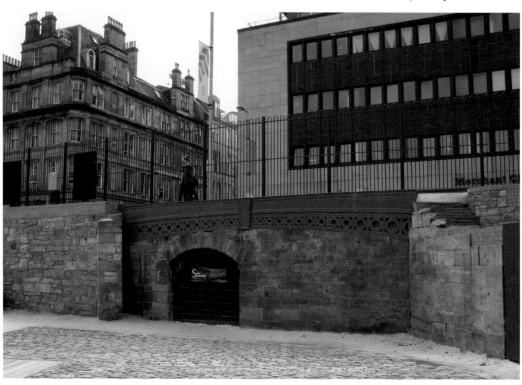

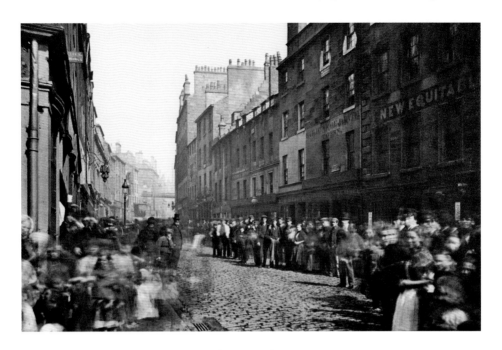

Saltmarket Shortly Before Wholesale Slum Clearance, *c.* 1870

Waulkergait, as Saltmarket was first known, was largely destroyed in the Great Fires of 1652 and 1677, and is another of Glasgow's oldest roads. It formed part of the route that linked the monastic community beside the Molendinar to the riverside. Saltmarket used to end at the Molendinar Burn, which blocked the route in medieval times, and traffic was diverted westwards to Glasgow Bridge via Bridgegait. It was only extended to the Clyde in the 1790s. One notable resident was Oliver Cromwell, who stayed for a time during his invasion of Scotland.

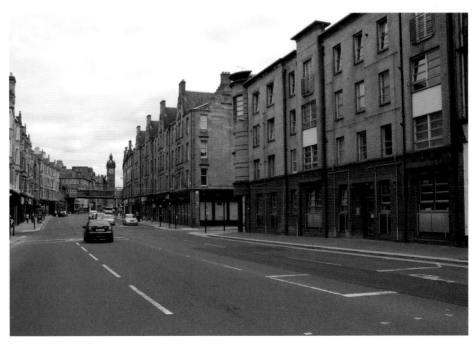

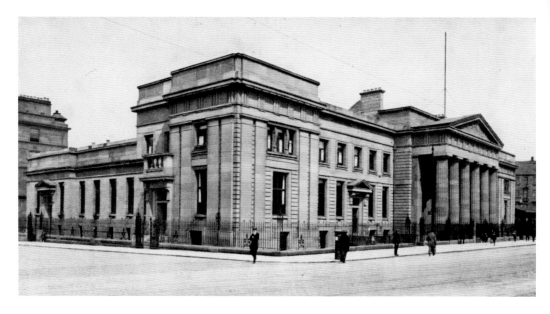

The Justiciary Courts in Saltmarket, Facing Glasgow Green

Originally accommodated in the Tolbooth until 1795, the Lords of Justiciary held court in a building in the High Street until the new court buildings were completed in 1814. Executions were carried out in front of the new building, giving rise to the cautionary expression of 'you'll die facing the monument' (meaning Nelson's monument in the Green). The last person to fulfill this prophecy was the murderer Dr Edward Pritchard in 1865. The new entrance to the High Court was opened up in Jocelyn Square in 1997.

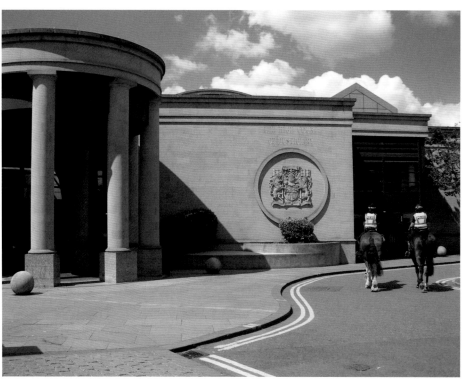

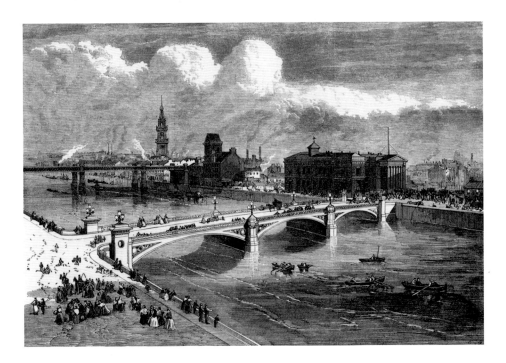

Albert Bridge

Albert Bridge was named after Queen Victoria's consort and opened in 1871. It was the fifth bridge to cross the Clyde to Hutchesontown from the Saltmarket area. During a riot on Glasgow Green in 1821, one earlier wooden structure collapsed. The present bridge is highly visible from the Green, where entertainments were provided during the 2014 Commonwealth Games. For that occasion, almost the entire structure was draped in vivid pink coverings, bearing one of the slogans of the Games – 'People Make Glasgow'.

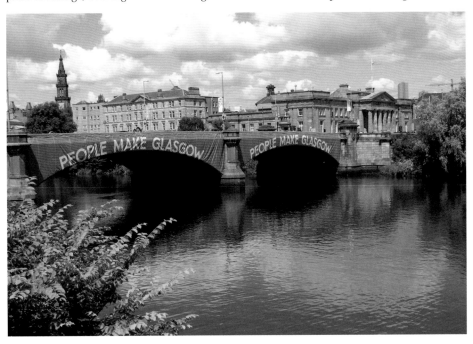

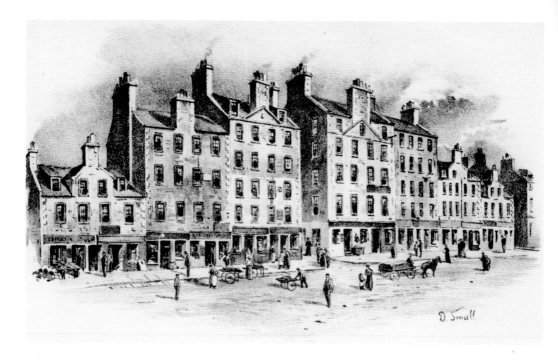

An Early Eighteenth-Century Sketch of the Gallowgate from Calton Mouth to Calton Entry
Calton was Glasgow's first industrial suburb and was founded in 1705. It was initially known as Blackfauld, not becoming Calton until around 1723. It was an independent burgh with its own Provost from 1815, until annexed by Glasgow in 1846. The Mouth and the Entry were the two main access routes into the Calton. The older tenements have all been replaced, as shown, and in the distance is the Barrowlands, located above the Barras. Once famed as Glasgow's premier dance hall, it is now a renowned live music venue.

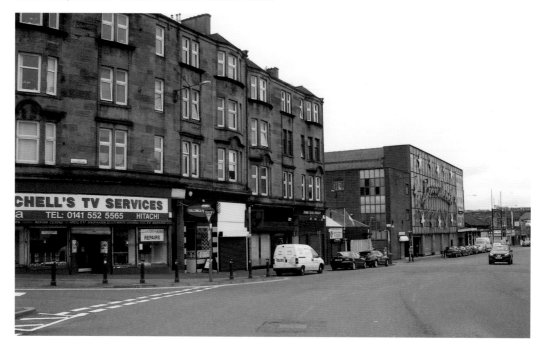

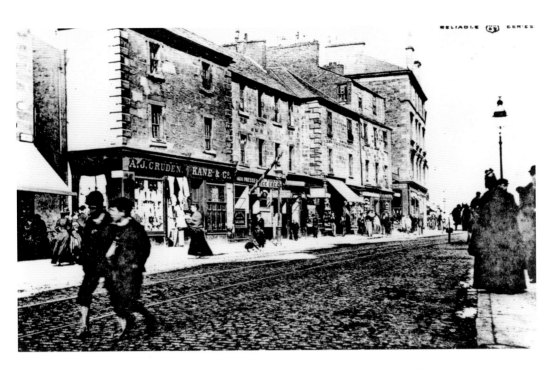

The Three Block Range of the Original Saracen Head Inn, Postcard *c.* 1906

The inn operated from 1755 to 1792 and had several claims to fame, some of which included accommodating Robert Burns, James Boswell and Dr Johnston. The Saracen Head public house opened in 1905 as the old inn buildings were being taken down, and is located at the corner of the furthest tenement in the above image. The pub now appears to have joined with many others in the vicinity in adopting the colours of the East End's most famous football club – Celtic.

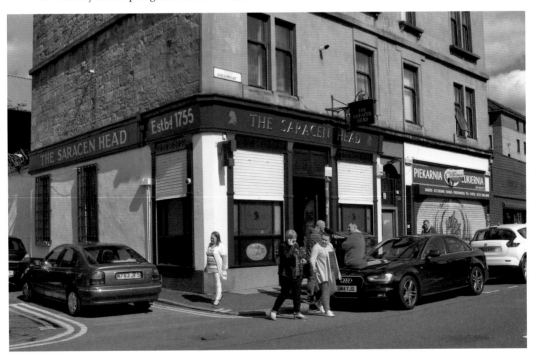

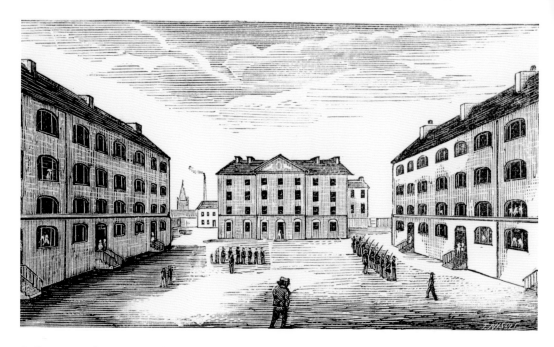

Gallowgate Infantry Barracks

In 1795, the barracks that accommodated 1,200 soldiers were built on the town's medieval butts, which had previously been used for archery practice. This was a relief to citizens, who were no longer required to provide billets for troops. The period was one of social unrest, with recent memories of the Weavers' Strike riots of 1787. The troops were intended to prevent any revolutionary uprisings. The barracks were removed to Maryhill c. 1874 and the priorities of the times have changed. One of Glasgow's most ancient sites is now given over to the public's demands for shopping and parking.

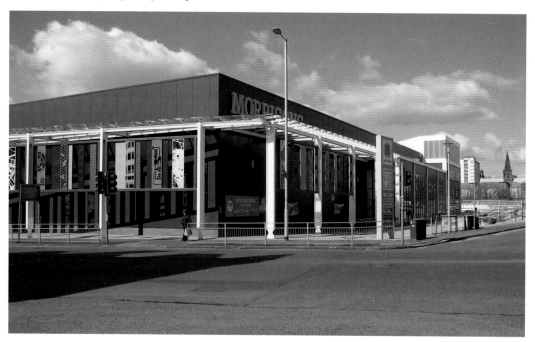

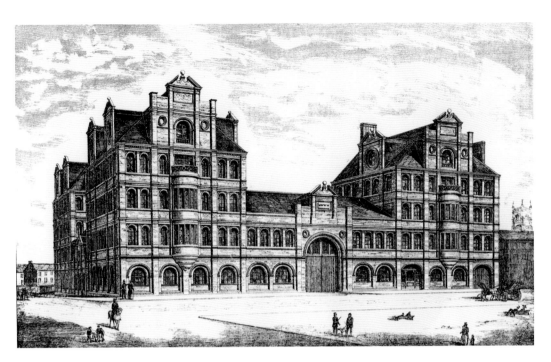

W. White & Son's Clay Pipe Factory, Facing into Bain Square, Calton, *c.* 1879
Bain Square was developed by the City Improvement Trust in the 1870s to help remove some of the worst areas of the Calton slums and create an open space for its inhabitants. Opposite St Luke's Church of Scotland, this factory was built in a French Renaissance style. Glaswegians were very fond of their pipes, and this was the largest of the manufacturers in the city. Much of the building has survived, although it has mostly been absorbed into the adjacent Barras.

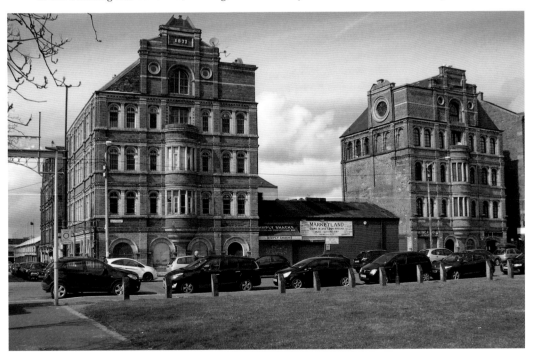

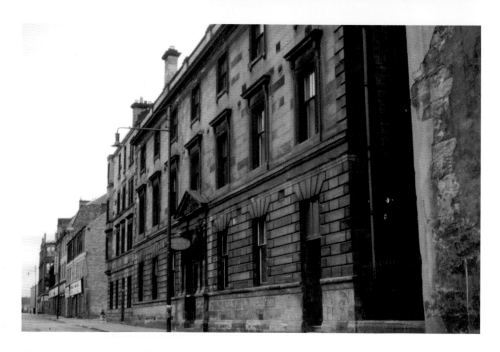

Moncur Street Lodging House for Women

Moncur Street Lodging House for Women, seen here in 1974, was situated in the heart of the Barras, in Calton. It was one of many hostels opened by Glasgow Corporation from the nineteenth century onwards to meet the needs of those who couldn't afford to rent a house. In later years they became home to the more marginalised and excluded members of our society. Glasgow's recent rehousing policy has seen the majority of these hostels closed, with their occupants provided with tenancies. The hostel operated from 1871 to 1983 and has now gone, but the Barras continues to operate as it has done for almost a century.

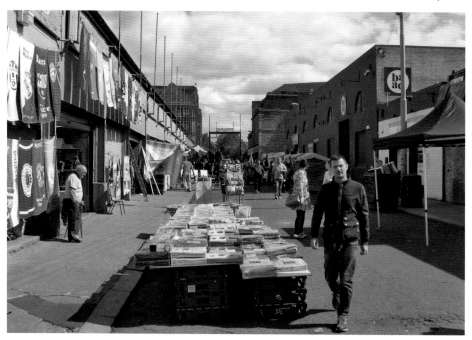

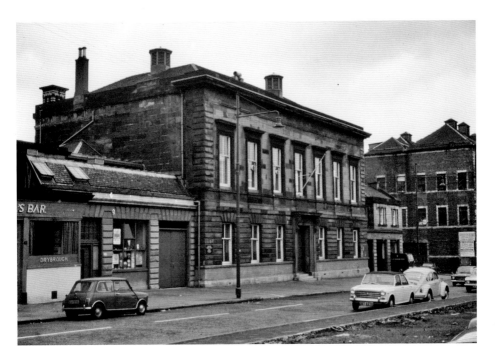

The Eastern District Police Station, Tobago Street, Calton, in 1974 and 2014
This police station is a survivor of the slum clearances in Glasgow. It accommodated not only the police, but also a court room and a fire station. It was built in 1868/69, but has been neglected for decades since policing moved to the new Eastern Division building in London Road in 1981. Calton had its own Baron's jail and police force when it became an independent burgh, but its jurisdiction terminated at the Calton boundary. It is suggested that arrest in Calton could be evaded by jumping over the Camlachie Burn into Bridgeton.

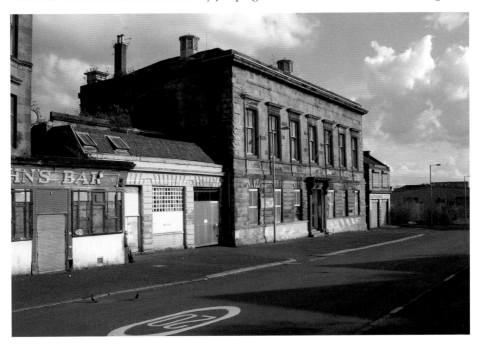

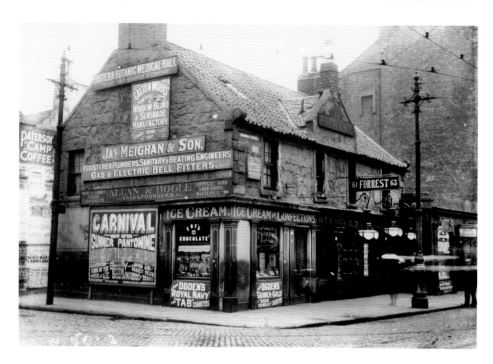

Glasgow Shopfronts

Our predecessors certainly required no lessons on the power of advertising if this shop is anything to go by. It was a survivor of the earliest architecture of Calton and Bridgeton from the late eighteenth century, and was located at the junction of Abercromby Street (then Clyde Street) and Canning Street (now London Road). Sadly, the shop was lost to posterity *c.* 1935 and replaced by a Royal Bank of Scotland. Latterly, the corner site has been taken up by a funeral services firm. This entry to Abercromby Street is now a cul-de-sac, ending at the gates to Calton Burying Ground.

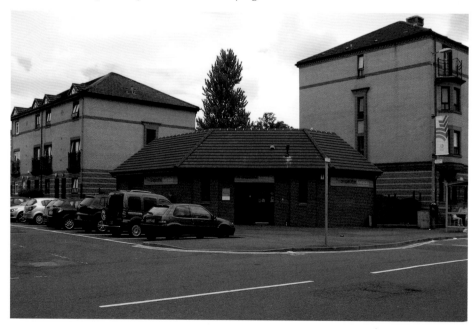

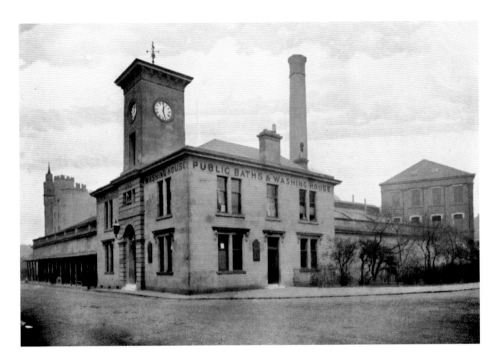

Greenhead Baths and Wash House, Greenhead Street at Templeton Street, Calton
As part of a response to address the poor health of the local population, Glasgow Corporation embarked upon a programme of building public baths and wash houses in the city. The first of these was the Greenhead Baths beside Glasgow Green, opened in 1878, which replaced the old wash house on the Green. A remarkable feature for Glasgow was the later addition of an outdoor swimming pool. The neighbouring Templeton's factory eventually encroached onto the site by 1960 and the baths were lost. Both have now been replaced by a new apartment block.

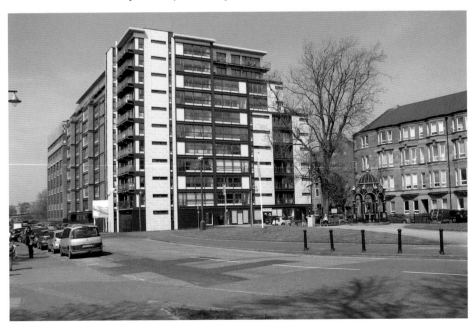

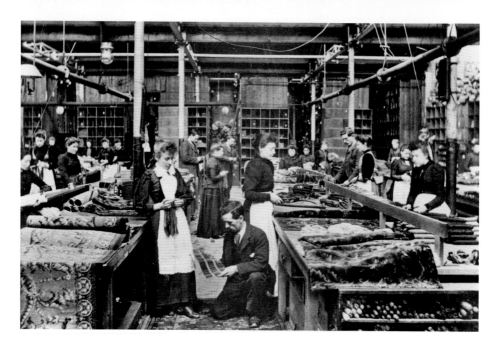

Templeton Factories

Templeton had several factories in the East End manufacturing its world-famous carpets. The above illustrates a sample room in their Crownpoint Carpet Works in Mile End around 1900. However, the undoubted jewel in the firm's crown was the factory built in Calton, facing Glasgow Green. It is said that Templeton had to produce an architectural design that would not adversely affect the amenity of the location. However, it was most probably in commemoration of the firm's founder, who died in 1885. Whatever the reason, the superb façade, which emerged in 1892, continues to adorn both the park and the city.

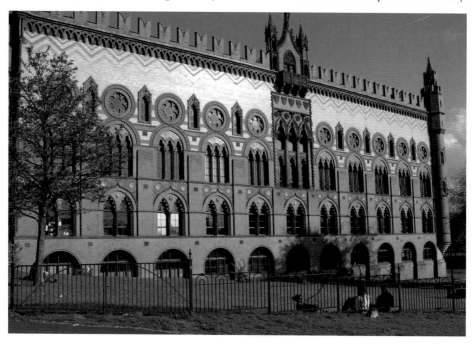

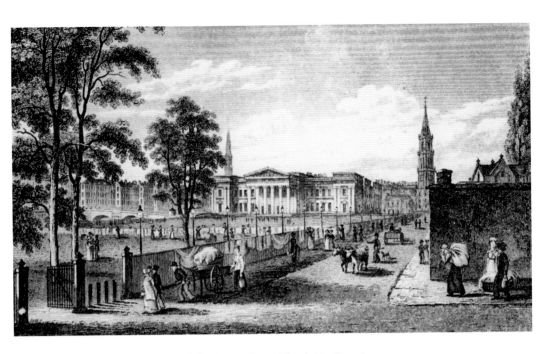

An 1826 View Along Greendyke Street from Charlotte Street

Glasgow Green and the Justiciary Buildings are also in the picture. Charlotte Street was laid out from 1780 as a fashionable place of residence, which, at one time, included the villa of philanthropist David Dale. The Green and the courts have not changed significantly since then, except for the growth of the intervening trees. In Greendyke Street, the remaining building of the one-time Our Lady & St Francis Secondary School now sits at the junction. Further along can be seen part of the 'Homes of the Future' complex of experimental designs, which opened in 1999 while Glasgow was UK City of Architecture.

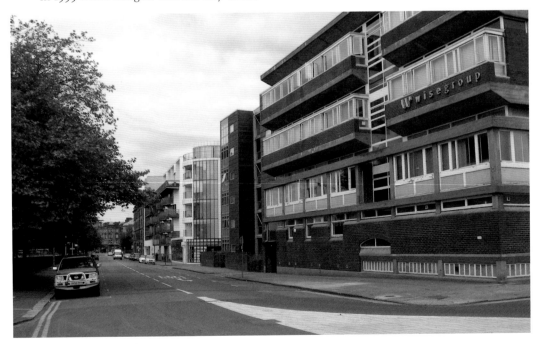

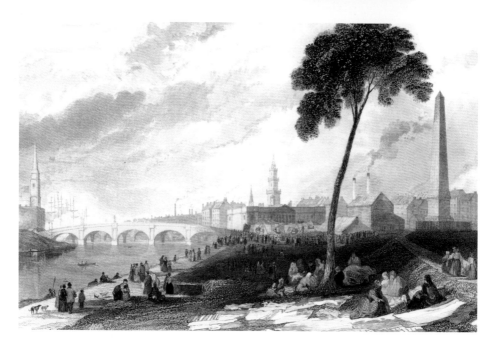

The Low Green

The Low Green in 1848 was very much a functional as well as a recreational space. While some people enjoyed leisure time strolling along the embankment to the fair, others were not so fortunate. Women toiled in the same area, washing and drying their laundry. Today it would be unthinkable to go to the Low Green to hang up your washing. The carnival continues its annual residence at varying locations on the Green during the modern Glasgow Fair fortnight. A predominant feature of the Low Green is Nelson's Monument, erected in 1806; the first in the United Kingdom to celebrate Nelson's historic victory at Trafalgar.

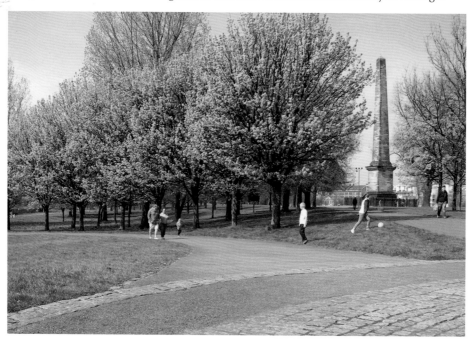

Glasgow Green's Moveable Monuments

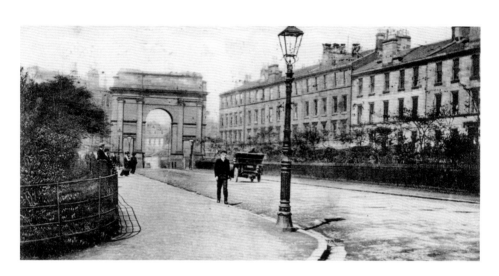

The McLennan Arch, c. 1900, Near Monteith Row

Glasgow's very own Arc de Triomphe now sits at the Saltmarket entrance to the Green, as seen in the 2014 photograph, framing Nelson's Monument. Originally part of the façade of the Athenaeum in Ingram Street, the central arch through which people now walk once framed a window. When the Athenaeum was taken down in 1892, the arch was saved by Baillie James McLennan, and reconstructed near the west end of Monteith Row. In 1922, it was moved again, to the end of Charlotte Street, then finally to its present location in 1991/92.

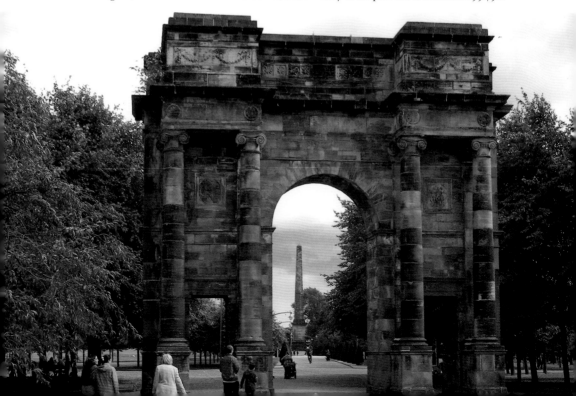

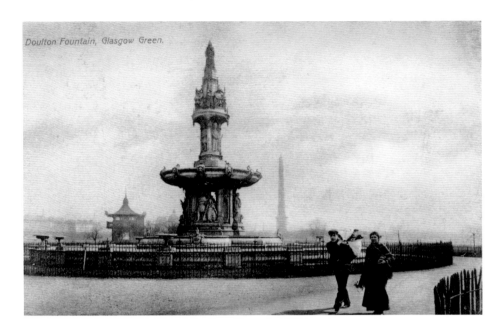

The Doulton Fountain, *c.* 1905

When it was produced by Doulton & Co. for the Glasgow Exhibition of 1888, this remarkable terracotta structure was reputedly the largest of its kind in the world. The fountain was gifted to the city and transferred to Glasgow Green in 1890, where it was sited between Nelson's Monument and the Justiciary Buildings. It fell into a state of major disrepair and was almost lost to posterity before steps were finally taken to restore it. Re-sited in front of the People's Palace Museum to protect it, the fountain was unveiled to the public in 2005.

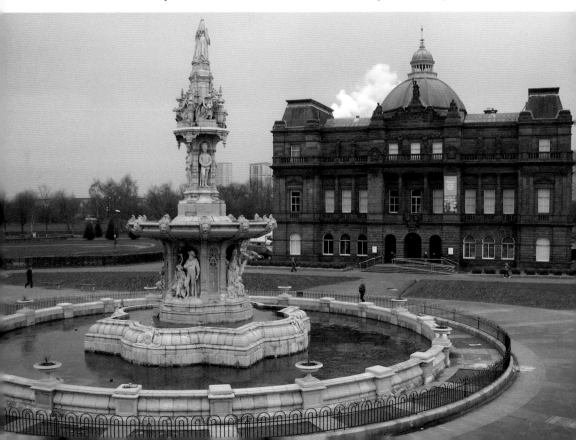

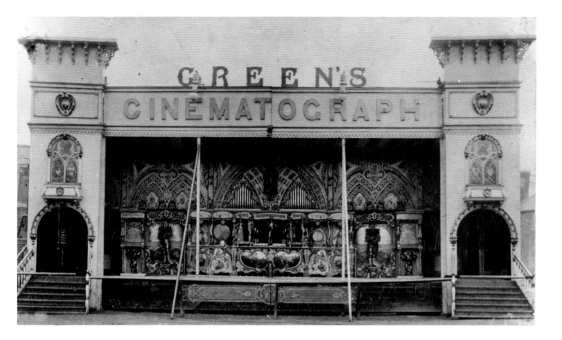

Green's Cinematograph

Green's Cinematograph was perceived as extremely high-tech when it was exhibited on Glasgow Green about 1906. George Green is credited as a pioneer in moving pictures with public performances held at fairgounds around the country in his mobile booths. For a penny or two, a twenty-minute show for up to 500 people at a time could be provided. Modern audiences have greater expectations. Entertainment on Glasgow Green has moved on, with giant screens routinely available to allow everyone to see what is happening on stage, as seen here during the 2014 Games – but is it as magical?

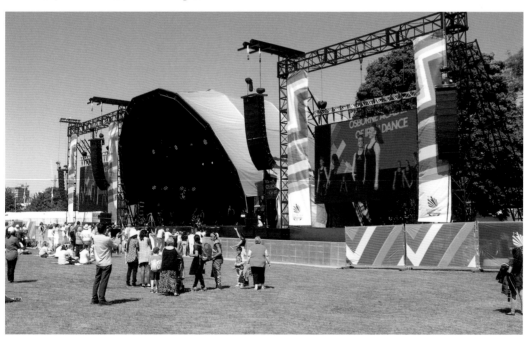

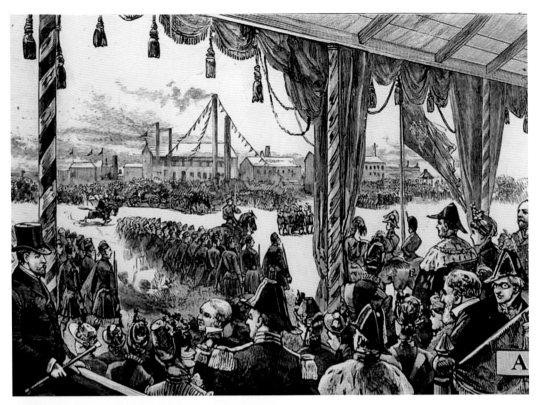

Glasgow Green

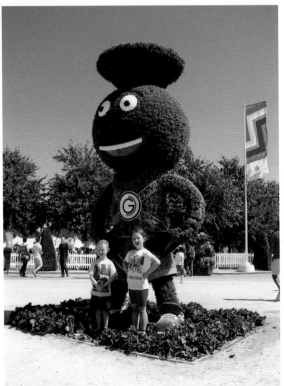

Glasgow Green has always been used for public meetings, recreational activities and displays of various kinds. Prince Charles Edward Stuart reviewed his army on the Fleshers' Haugh when it occupied Glasgow in 1746. In 1887, Queen Victoria's Golden Jubilee was celebrated with a review of 10,000 troops and volunteers, as shown above. When Glasgow hosted the Commonwealth Games, the Green was employed for a less martial celebration. Copies of the Games mascot, Clyde, were deployed around the city, and this one on the Green, at the previous site of the Doulton Fountain, provided a photograph opportunity for visitors and Glaswegians alike.

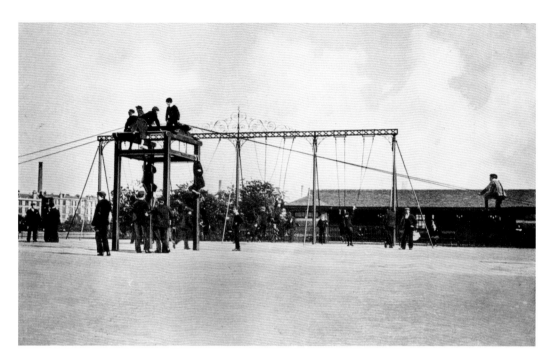

Outdoor Gymnasium

An outdoor gymnasium was constructed by Glasgow Corporation on the Green near James Street, *c.* 1900. It was a fairly basic sporting provision, with all the accompanying risks of falling onto a hard surface. Even the red gravel on the Provost Haugh football pitches, which scraped the skin off generations of footballers, or turned to mud when it rained, has been replaced with grass. Beside the new pitches on the Haugh is the most recent addition to the Green – the National Hockey Centre.

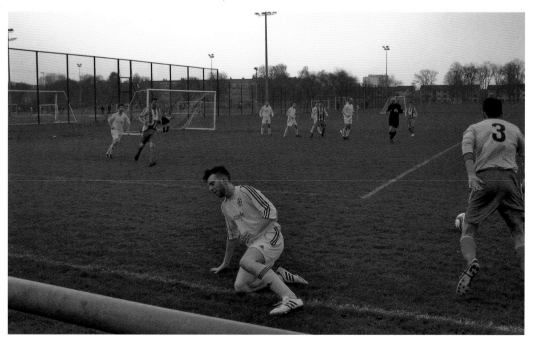

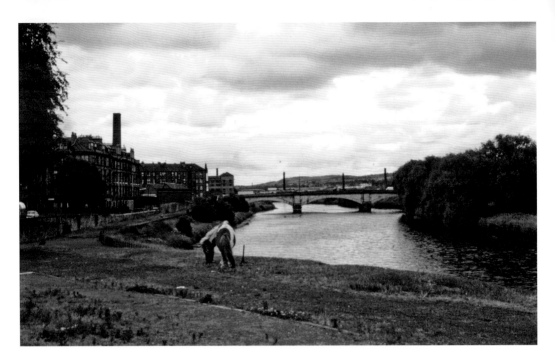

A Pony

A pony belonging to the carnival folk grazes on common land in 1974. For a significant period of time, the carnival was banished to the football pitches at Provost Haugh. There, it was a much anticipated prelude to the annual evacuation of the East End for the Fair fortnight holidays. In the background are the tenements of Newhall and Rutherglen Bridge. It was there that Allan's Pen was built, impeding access to the riverside footpath, much to the anger of locals. Only the bridge remains to identify the location of the earlier photograph.

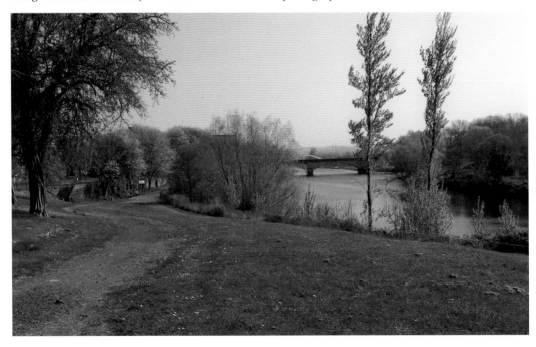

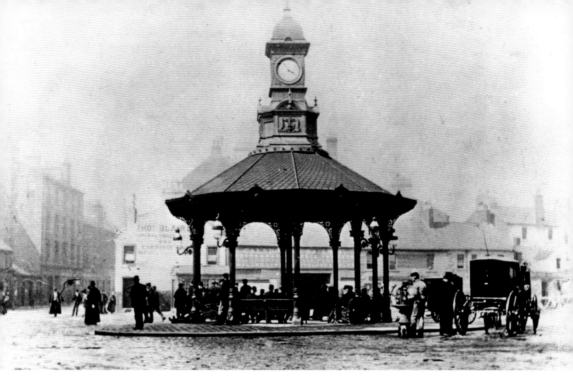

The Umbrella at Bridgeton Cross *c.* 1894

This was erected in 1875 as a shelter and meeting place by the Sun Foundry. Bridgeton originated in 1776 with the construction of Rutherglen Bridge. It was initially known as Bridgetown, and was established on the extensive Barrowfield estate. The first Bridgeton Cross was simply marked by stones in the road at the crossroads of Reid Street and Dale Street. However, in the late 1870s, the City Improvement Trust created the present Bridgeton Cross at Barrowfield Toll, with the Umbrella as the centrepiece of the new creation.

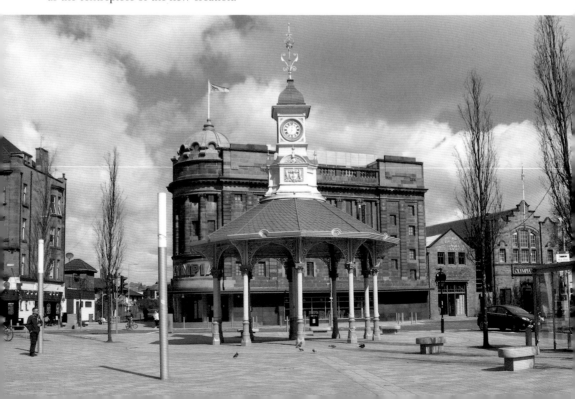

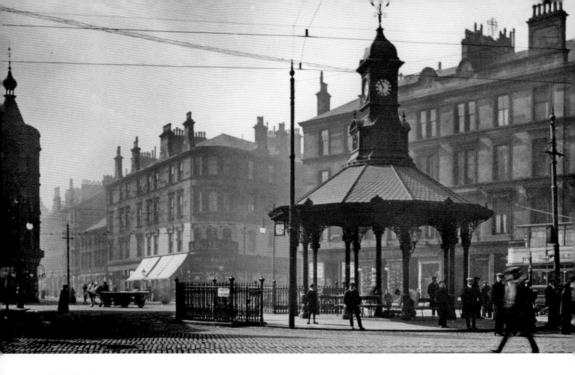

GEAR Project

Today, 100 years later, Bridgeton Cross and adjacent properties were designated as a Core Area by GEAR (the Glasgow East Area Renewal). GEAR preserved it during an extensive period of slum clearance, when almost everything else surrounding the core was being demolished. One part that could not be saved was the south-eastern corner between Main Street and James Street. This once housed the locally well-known Logie's department store with its pneumatic tube payment transfer system, which certainly fascinated the younger customers. The small shopping mall that replaced it has met with only limited success over the years.

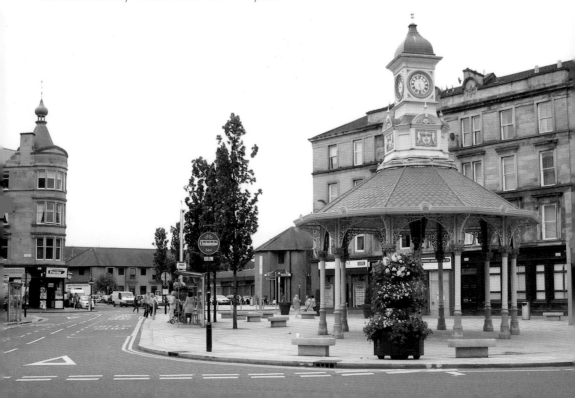

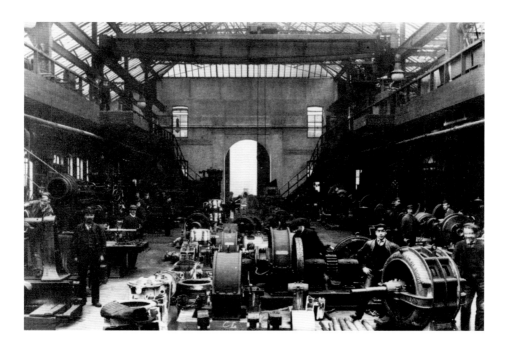

Mavor & Coulson's Works

This image shows large electrical motors being built at Mavor & Coulson's works in Broad Street, Mile End, in 1906. This electrical engineering works started on the site of the Olympia in 1881, moving to Broad Street in 1892. It introduced the first public electricity supply in the country for Glasgow Corporation and later pioneered mining equipment. The company ended as part of the Anderson Group, when the country's mining industry collapsed in the 1990s. Its office block, shown below, is now used as Park Lane House. Mile End was a heavily industrialised area, and even now it has very little residential property.

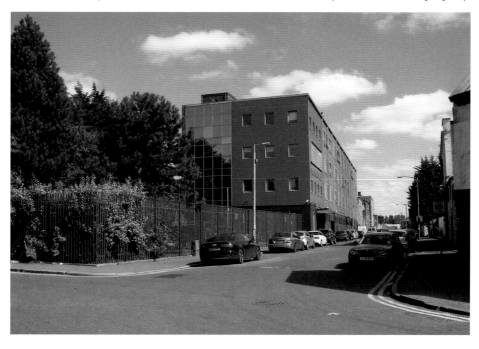

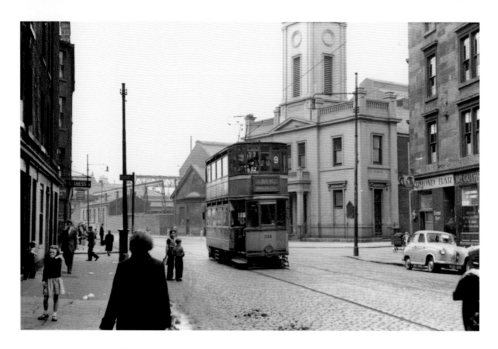

A No. 9 Tram Heading to Dalmuir West from London Road

The image shows the junction with Brook Street, Mile End. The church was built for a Secession congregation in 1837 as London Road Church of Scotland, and the site is now occupied by the Gulf filling station. In the distance is the engineering complex, which started as Duncan Stewart & Co.'s London Road Ironworks, and ended as Davy United. Brook Street takes its name from the Camlachie Burn, which runs beneath the street on its way through Bridgeton Cross to the Clyde. This burn formed the boundary between Bridgeton and neighbouring Mile End and Calton.

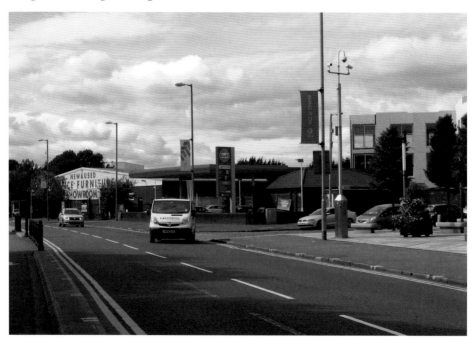

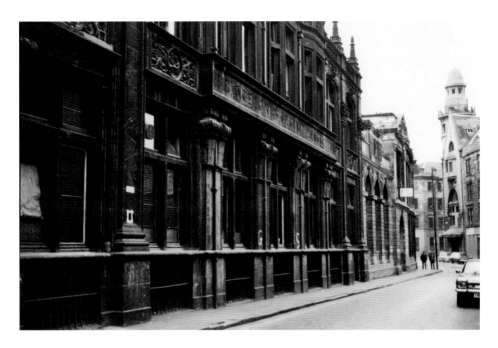

Landressy Street

Little remains of the significant architecture that once graced Landressy Street, seen here around 1975. One of Bridgeton's oldest streets, it accommodated the Bridgeton Working Men's Club, the Methodist Central Hall, Bridgeton Masonic Hall and Bridgeton West & Barrowfield Church of Scotland. The only remnant is the beautiful Carnegie library of 1906. Now home to the Glasgow Women's Library, its original functions have transferred to the one-time Theatre of Variety and cinema to the Olympia building on Bridgeton Cross. The old picture house was rescued from a lingering demise by the intervention of Clyde Gateway and given a new lease of life.

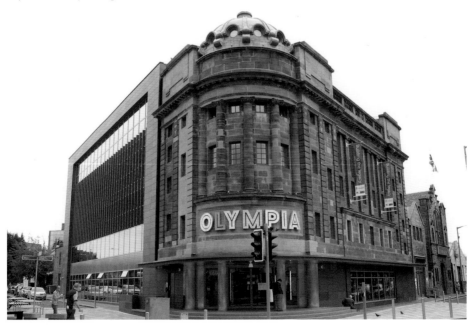

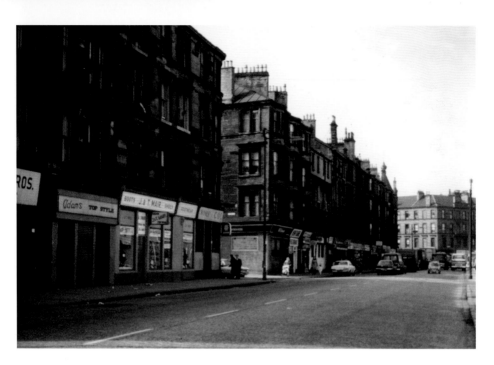

Dalmarnock Road Toward Bridgeton Cross at its Junction with Acorn Street in 1975
This road was formed on part of the ancient route that stonemasons from Rutherglen used to take when walking to their work at the cathedral in medieval times. The distance from the ford at Dalmarnock to the Camlachie Burn was approximately 1 mile, and beneath most of its length now runs a railway tunnel between Bridgeton and Dalmarnock railway stations. Some of the Victorian tenements shown above were demolished during the late 1970s during GEAR, and replaced by the housing seen below.

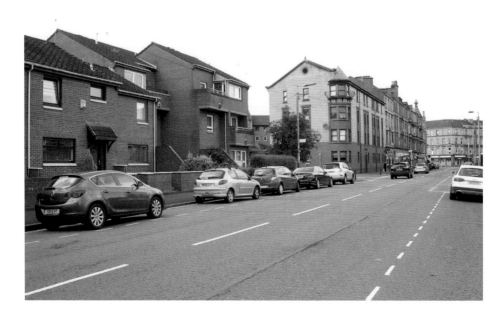

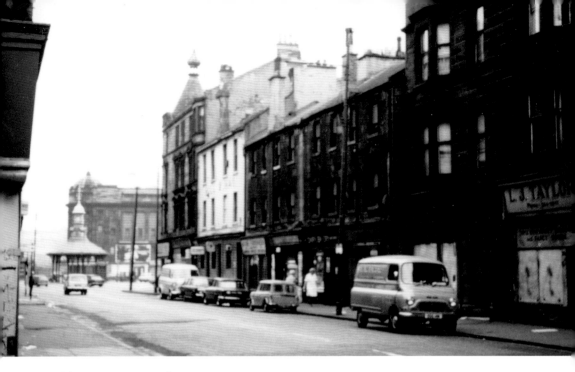

Bridgeton Cross Mansions

The spire of Bridgeton Cross Mansions marks the meeting point of Dalmarnock Road and Main Street in 1974. Main Street linked Barrowfield Toll to Rutherglen Bridge, along which the community of Bridgeton developed after 1776. Some of its earliest streets, named for individuals such as Benjamin Franklin, indicate a radical tradition frequently associated with the district thereafter. When Bridgeton was annexed to Glasgow in 1846, it retained the name of its principal street. Once a thriving and bustling residential and commercial area, the changes made to Bridgeton during the activities of GEAR reduced the population hugely, resulting in a comparatively tranquil but relatively uninteresting district.

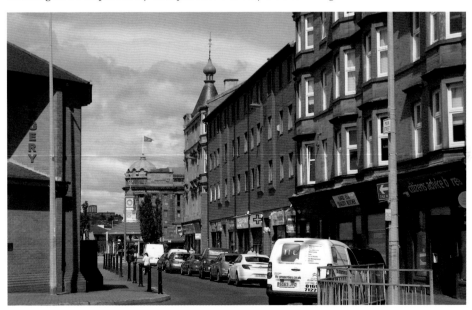

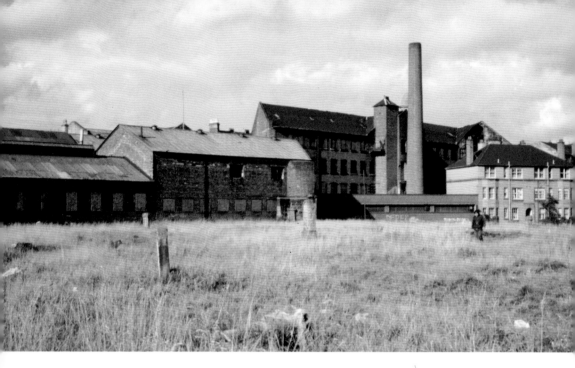

Bridgeton Burying Ground

A few isolated headstones poke through the crab grass in Bridgeton Burying Ground, Tullis Street, shown here in 1974. This graveyard was associated with the first church to be built in the village in 1806 – Bridgeton Relief Church – in what was then John Street. By 1974, this sad scene of dereliction was set to a backdrop of disused factories on James Street, but, within a few years, it was converted into a recreational space at the time of GEAR. The memorial stones were relocated to the boundary walls. The graveyard was further restored and landscaped by Clyde Gateway in 2009, renamed as the Tullis Street Memorial Gardens.

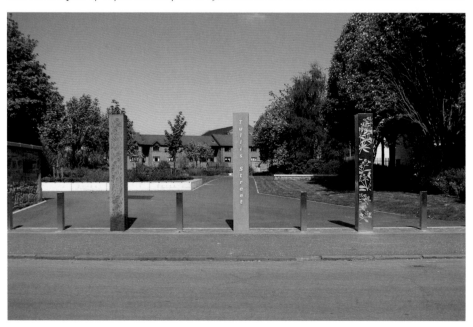

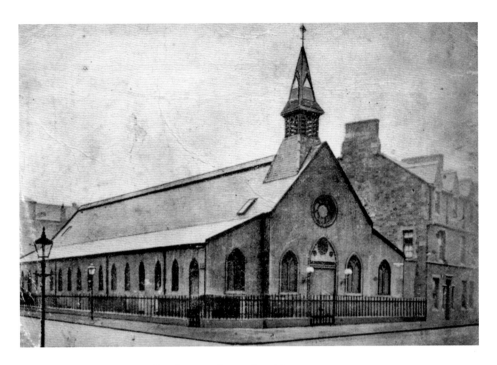

Sacred Heart Mission, Old Dalmarnock Road, Bridgeton

Despite the widespread antipathy towards them at the time, Catholics were present in Bridgeton from its earliest days. It was not until 1873 that the Sacred Heart Mission from St Mary's was established in the district. A temporary church was built in Old Dalmarnock Road to be replaced in 1909/10, with the present highly ornate and impressive edifice in the architectural style and dimensions of a Roman basilica. It remains one of the few significant buildings to have survived the GEAR ravages of the district in the 1970s.

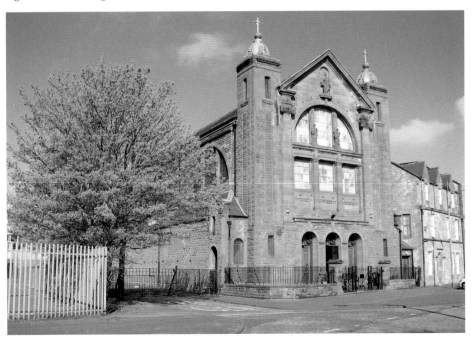

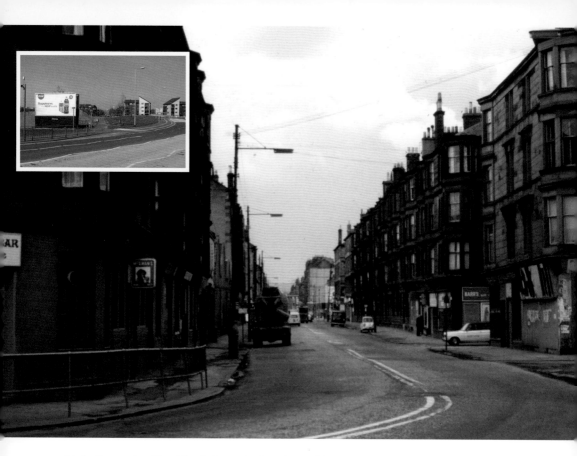

Main Street, Looking North from Rutherglen Bridge, 1974 and 2014
Main Street is barely recognisable since this photograph was taken forty years ago. With pedestrianisation of the Cross and the southern part of the route largely diverted to east and west, little traffic – motorised or pedestrian – now passes along the old road. A barely noticeable pavement marks the entrance to this one-time main artery of village life, the venue for an almost continuous series of shops, cinemas and small businesses on either side. Main Street is now almost entirely residential, with traditional tenements now found mostly at Bridgeton Cross.

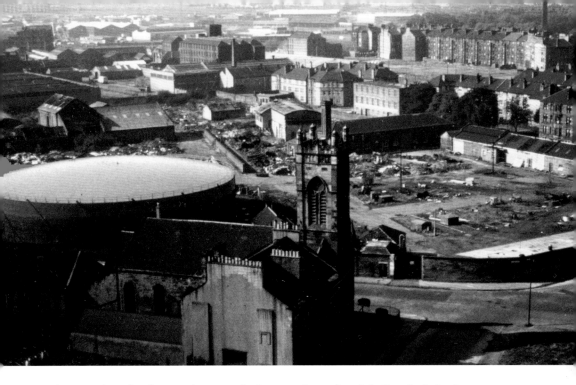

The Remains of Dalmarnock Gasworks in 1974, from the High Flats in Ruby Street
Dalmarnock hosted a remarkable number of public service industries – gas, electricity, water supply and sewage – but only the latter now remains. The works were built on Morgan's farm in 1843 by the City & Suburban Gas Co. and extended over the years to meet demand. Production ceased in 1956. The recent photograph, taken from the opposite direction, shows part of the recovered site, with the public sculpture of a circle of girders echoes the circle of the gas holder in the earlier image. In the distance are the Ruby Street flats.

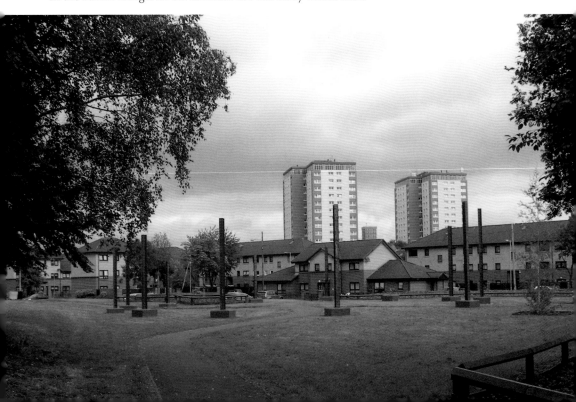

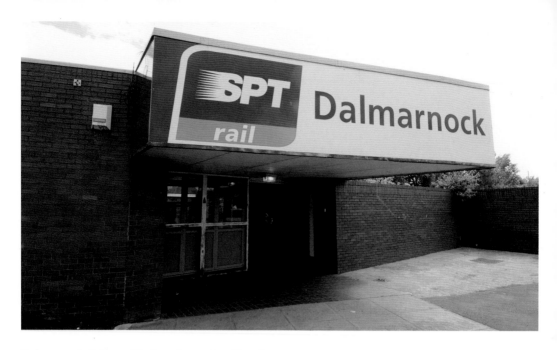

Dalmarnock Railway Station, Swanston Street

An overwhelming canopy above a rather underwhelming old entrance to the Dalmarnock station in Swanston Street. In stark contrast is the futuristic design of the new main entrance on Dalmarnock Road, sited near to where the original and ornate red sandstone entrance once stood. The station was renovated to meet the anticipated demands of the crowds who would be attending the nearby Commonwealth Games venues. At the same time, the spur-line railway bridge over Dalmarnock Road was removed to facilitate building the Clyde Gateway route from Rutherglen Bridge to Celtic Park.

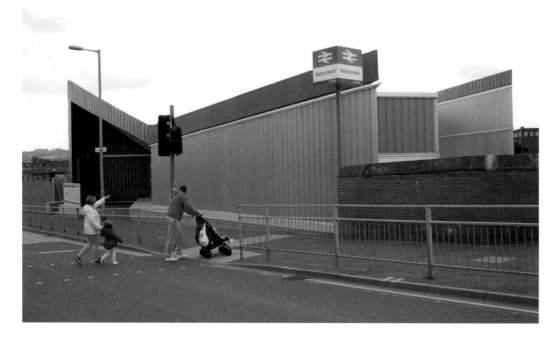

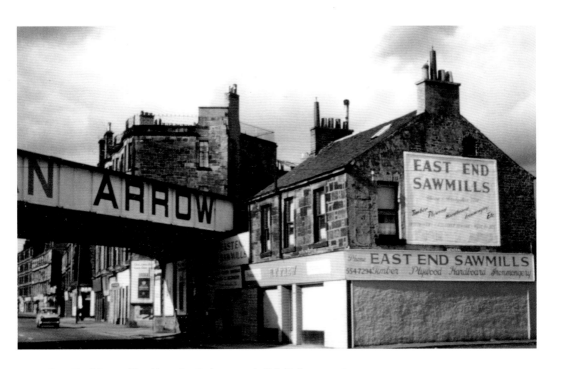

East End Sawmills, No. 367, Dalmarnock Rd, Dalmarnock, 1974
This was one of the earliest houses in Dalmarnock, dating from around the beginning of the nineteenth century. It is typical of the weavers' and miners' houses of the period. It is difficult to locate now as none of the buildings shown have survived, but it used to sit opposite the new railway station. It ended its days as part of the larger East End Sawmills Company, which moved across the river to Rutherglen. In marked contrast, and skipping the entire history of tenement development, is one of the newest houses at the Athletes' Village.

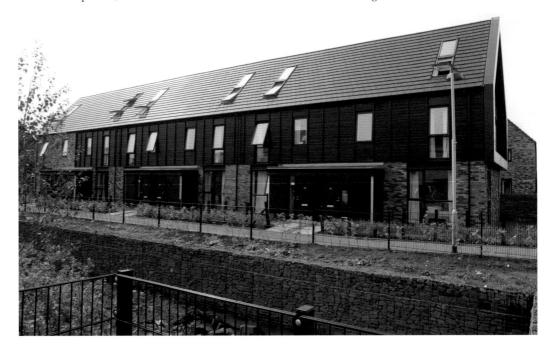

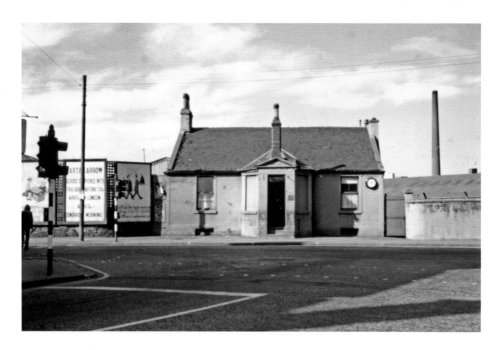

The 1820 Tollhouse

The tollhouse, shown here in 1974, was a notable feature of Dalmarnock Road, facing into Springfield Road. It was inexplicably demolished some years later. It seems extraordinary that the political will could not be found to preserve one of the very few vestiges of Dalmarnock's older history, and seems typical of the general lack of initiative to preserve the East End's architectural heritage. Originally built by the Road Trustees to collect tolls to facilitate further road building, its purpose was long ago superseded by other means. The building of the Clyde Gateway route, shown here in 2014, needed no such facility.

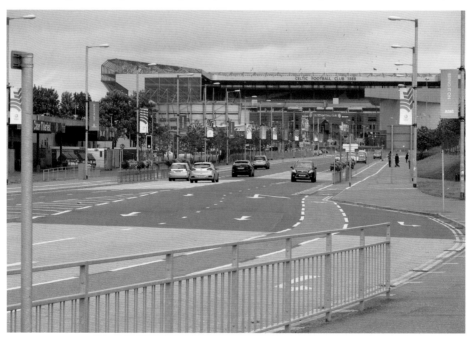

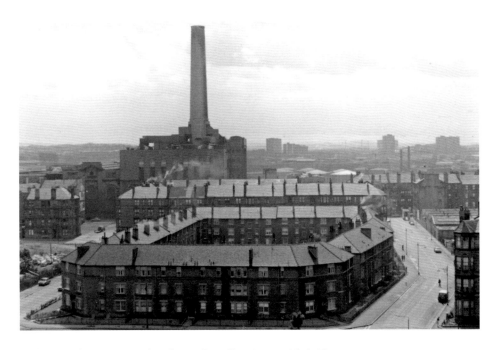

Dalmarnock Power Station from the Allan Street High Flats

Captured at Millerfield, Dalmarnock in the late 1970s. Almost all of the inter-war housing seen here was replaced during GEAR, as well as the older tenements. Dalmarnock Power Station was built from 1915, closed in 1977 and was finally demolished in 1980/81. In the preparation of the site for redevelopment by Clyde Gateway, it was discovered that the substructures had just been filled in, and therefore needed to be removed – an unexpected, expensive and arduous task. The site has now been turned into a green sward with a SUDS (Sustainable Urban Drainage System) pond to the west.

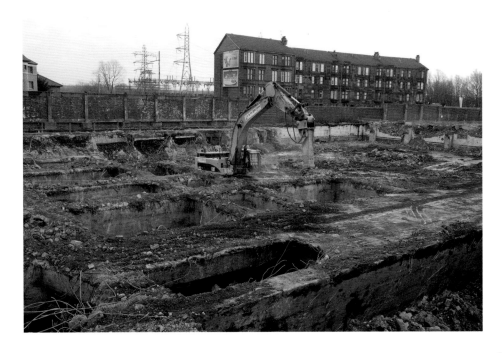

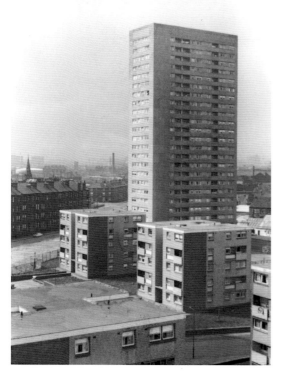

The High Flats on the Millerfield Estate Looking South-West From Allan Street, *c.* 1970
The four blocks of flats and accompanying maisonettes were built in the early 1960s. Along with most of the surviving traditional tenements, they were taken down to enable the construction of the Athletes' Village for the Commonwealth Games. The part of the village shown below, with its SUDs ponds, was occupied by the New Zealand team. In the foreground is a *pou whenua,* which in Maori culture marks boundaries. The team gifted two of these to the city in thanks for its hospitality when the Games ended.

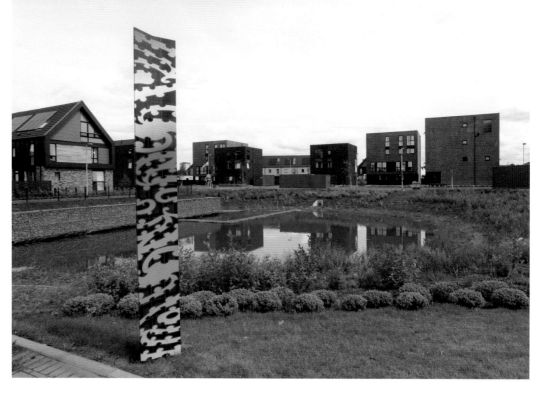

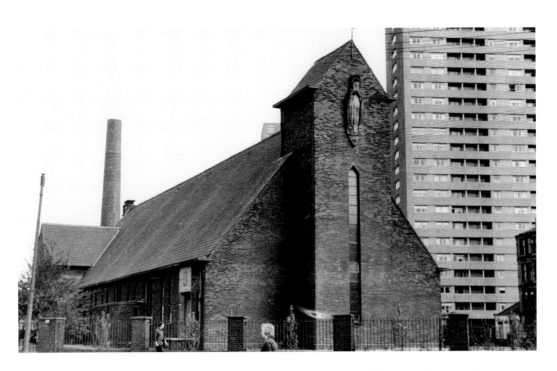

The RC Church of Our Lady of Fatima at the Junction of Springfield and Millerfield Roads, 1975
This parish was established in 1950, with the church built immediately afterwards, and terminated in 2004. The cleared site was used to provide temporary facilities for the athletes during the 2014 Games, and included a dining hall and a version of Nessie emerging from the lawn in front, which may or may not be retained. The buildings seen to the left of the Commonwealth flags are permanent and will form part of the new Glasgow City residential care home, which is being constructed at Springfield Road.

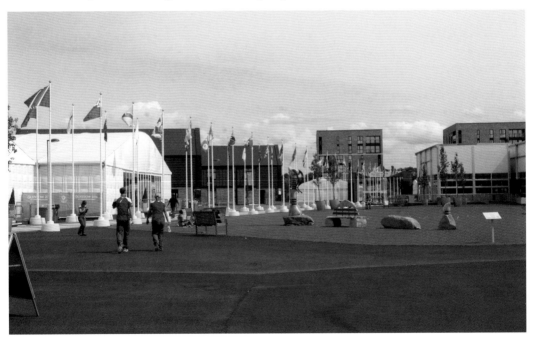

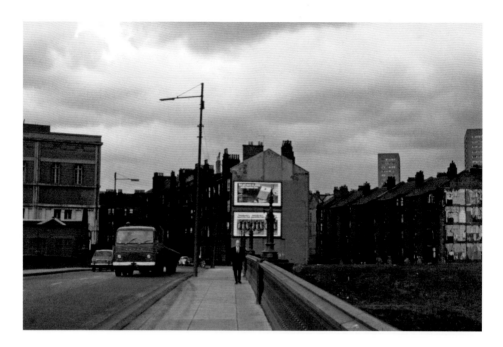

Dalmarnock Bridge

Entry to Dalmarnock from the Rutherglen side of the River Clyde via Dalmarnock Bridge. The original crossing was at a ford across the river at this spot, with the most recent bridge being constructed from 1893–96. To the left, the power station walls loomed over Dalmarnock Road, as did the tenements to the right. The canyon formed between them presented a rather intimidating entrance to the city. The impression gained from walking between the serried ranks of tenements can no longer be experienced in most parts of the East End. The sentinels remaining at the bridge since 1974 are the last traditional tenements in Dalmarnock.

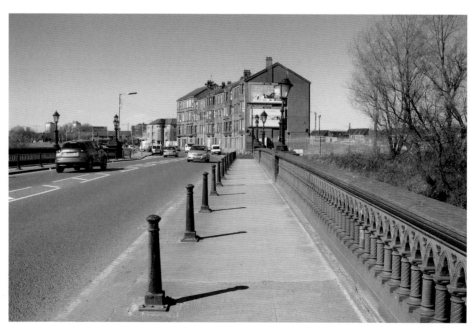

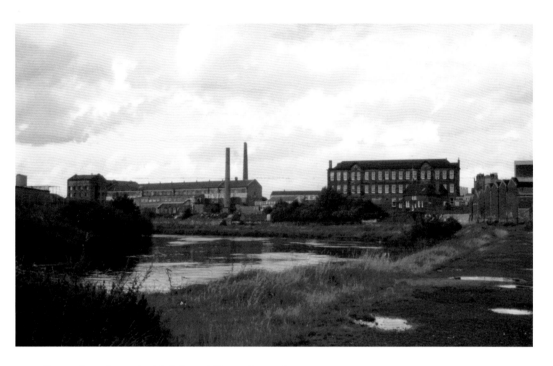

Downriver from the Vicinity of Shore Street in 1974

With Cowan's Chocolate Factory and Strathclyde School. Cowan's factory has gone but the school building remains in use. The most significant change is the construction of the new pedestrian bridge from Solway Street across to a walkway in Shawfield. The new bridge is as yet unnamed, and is intended to facilitate foot traffic from the new housing in the Athletes' Village. The public right of way along the north bank of the river, which was secured in 1828 as a result of the famous Harvey's Dyke case, is now part of the Clyde Walkway.

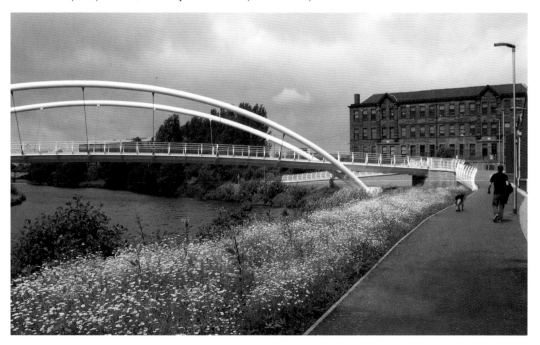

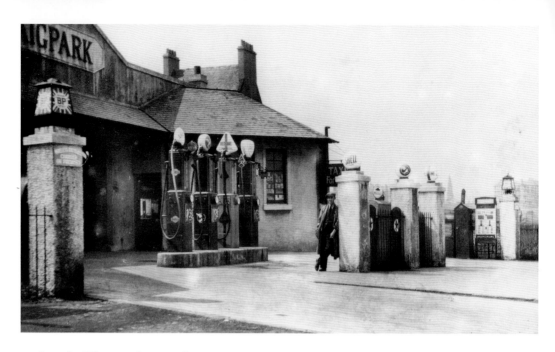

Craigpark Filling Station on Alexandra Parade c. 1930s,
The Spire of Glasgow Cathedral is just in view. Such small businesses can no longer meet the demands of modern motorists, who seem to expect a shopping experience when buying their petrol. BP still maintains a station on the site. This is overshadowed by the bulk of the huge late Art Deco WD & HQ Wills tobacco factory and warehouse which was built from 1946–53 and is now an office complex called City Park. This factory, with other tobacco companies in the locality, provided the nickname of Tobacco Land to the East End of Alexandra Parade.

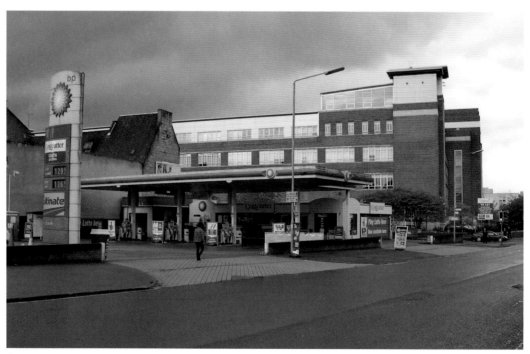

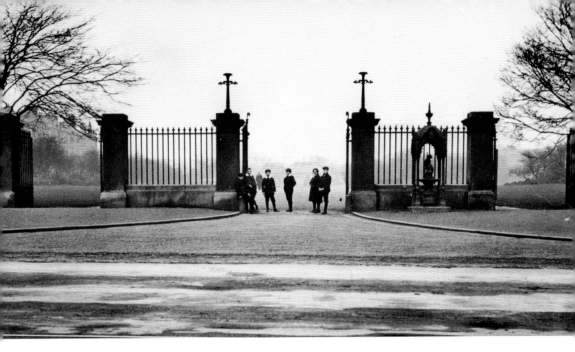

A Cold Winter's Day at the Alexandra Parade Entrance to Alexandra Park, Dennistoun
The park was laid out by the City Improvement Trust in 1866–70 to improve the attractiveness of the new Dennistoun suburb. The site on Wester Kennyhill was described at the time as bleak and windswept, and there were some doubts as to whether the park could survive. However, it did, thanks to the skills of its gardeners. The contrast here is the relative austerity of a winter day in around 1900, and the profusion of colourful flora that a 2014 summer can bring.

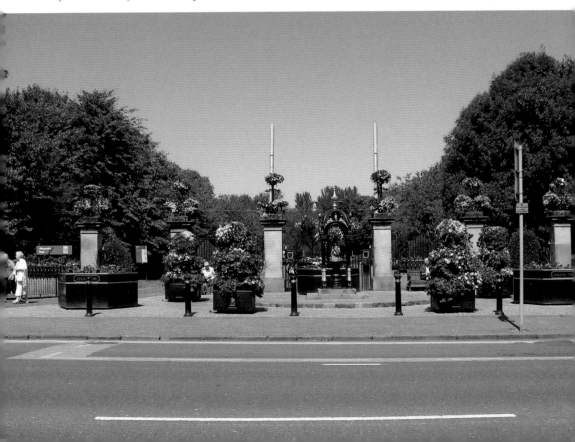

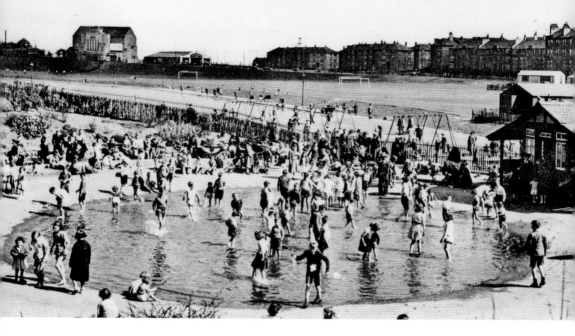

Alexandra Park

Like all Glasgow parks, Alexandra Park contained numerous recreational facilities for the public. One is a golf course, which was laid out on the drumlin to the north and is still in use today. A boating pond has now been reserved for the exclusive use of the wildlife. Another feature was the paddling pool – always a surprising element in some of the city's parks given the vagaries of a Glasgow summer. Obviously photographed here on a good day (*c.* 1930), what limited appeal there was has gone and the pond has been converted into a children's playground.

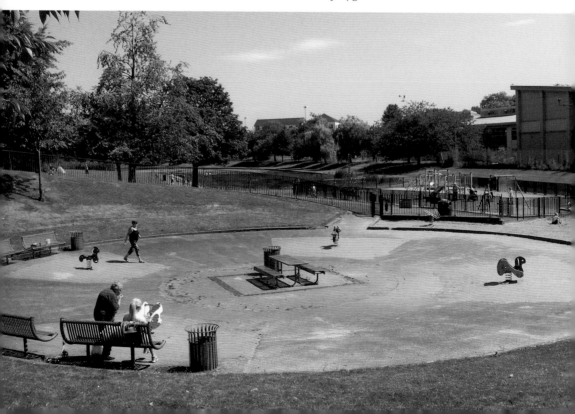

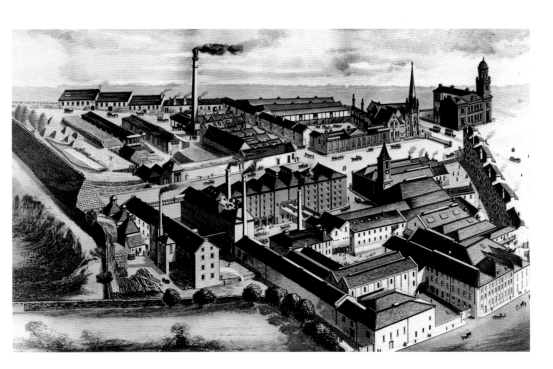

A Nineteenth-Century View of Tennent's Wellpark Brewery, with the Necropolis to the Left
The Tennent family have had a brewing connection with Glasgow since 1556, and opened premises at a site near the Drygate Bridge over the Molendinar in 1740. The brewery has expanded eastwards over the years and swallowed up a number of properties, including most of Ladywell Street. The above image has been reproduced as a tile mural at the Duke Street entrance, and some of the older buildings can be detected in the centre of the 2014 photograph.

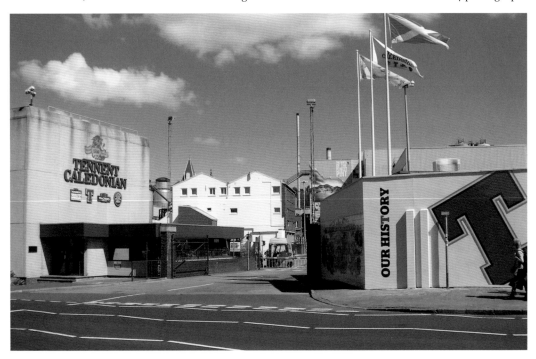

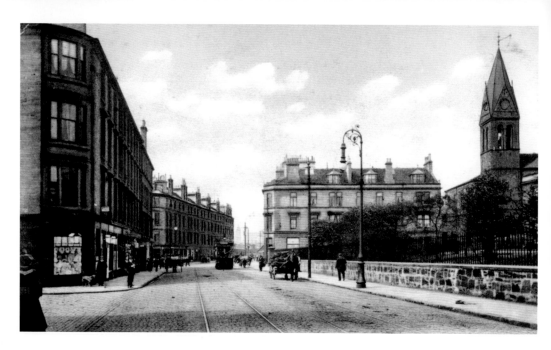

Westwards Along Duke Street Towards King's Cross at Westercraigs, Dennistoun, 1906
The Victorians were very fond of creating Crosses to ascribe status to an area. Surprisingly, little has changed in this vicinity in the past 100 years, except for the demolition of some tenements in the middle distance. This reflects the situation in much of Dennistoun, which is the only district in the East End to have retained a significant part of its architectural heritage. One alteration has been to Blackfriars church in Westercraigs. This has been converted into housing, while incorporating modifications to the exterior to produce an engaging Italianate effect.

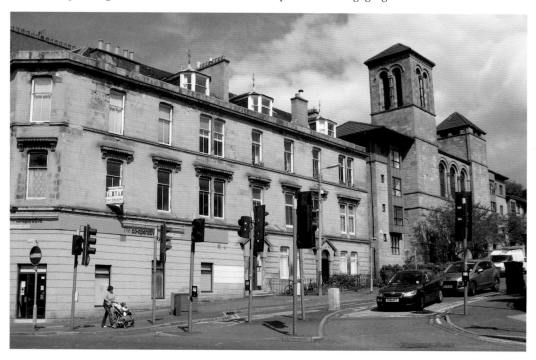

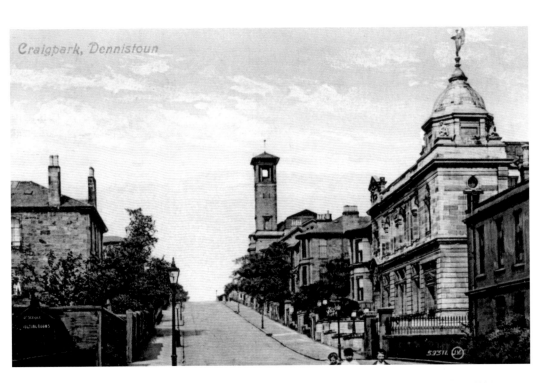

Craigpark, Dennistoun

Craigpark with
Dennistoun Public
Library and the
Tower of Regent Place
Church Beyond, 1900
The library was built
in 1905, and is one of
three in the East End
funded by Andrew
Carnegie, the others
being in Bridgeton
and Parkhead.
The building was
constructed on an
incline, and the
elaborate façade
can be better seen
in the recent front
elevation drawing by
Gerry Blaike (*shown
to the left*). The
church was built for
a United Presbyterian
congregation in 1877
and ended its days
as an assembly hall
for Whitehill School.
It was destroyed in a
fire in 1983.

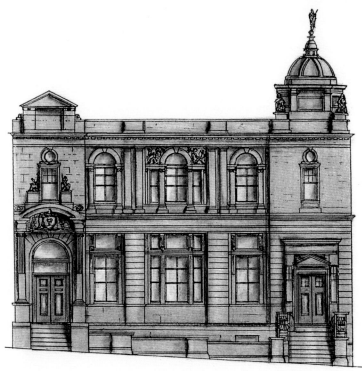

DENNISTOUN LIBRARY, 1905

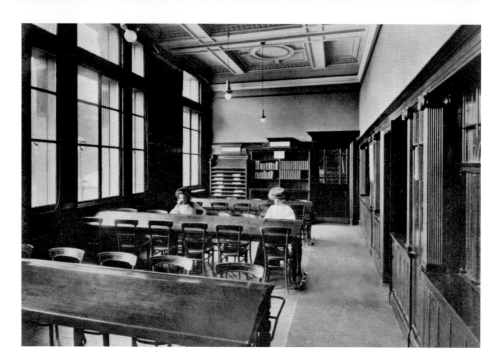

Interior Views of Dennistoun Public Library, 1914 and 2014

When the library opened, the social conventions of the period before the First World War allowed for the creation of a separate Ladies Reading Room, which has now been given over to general use. The library has had to move with the times to meet the changing needs of its users, and never more so than in recent decades. Below are the computer stations, which now provide the opportunity to access a breadth and depth of information that no single library can be expected to encompass on its bookshelves.

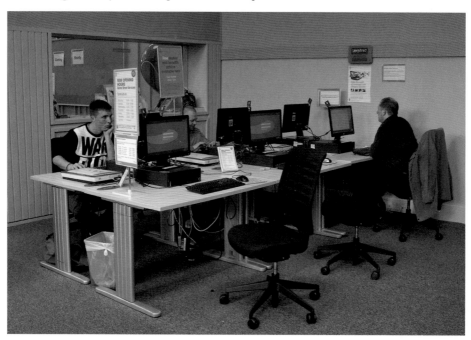

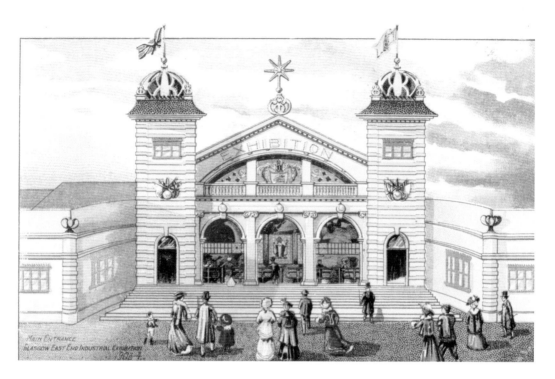

MAIN ENTRANCE
GLASGOW EAST END INDUSTRIAL EXHIBITION

Buffalo Bill Cody

It surprises most Glaswegians to hear that Buffalo Bill Cody actually visited their city in person. In fact, he did so twice between October 1891 and February 1892, when his Wild West Show was staged in the East End Exhibition Buildings in Dennistoun. The legacy of the visits included a number of the Sioux who remained in Scotland, a local gang taking the name of the Dennistoun Redskins (which could not have been coincidental) and a statue of Cody – beyond reach – on a plinth recently erected near the site of the shows in the grounds of the old Whitehill School.

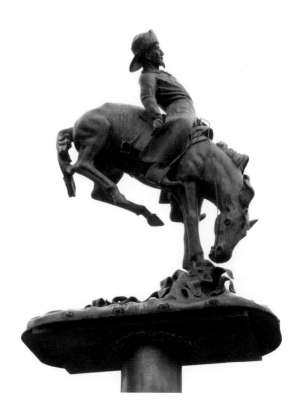

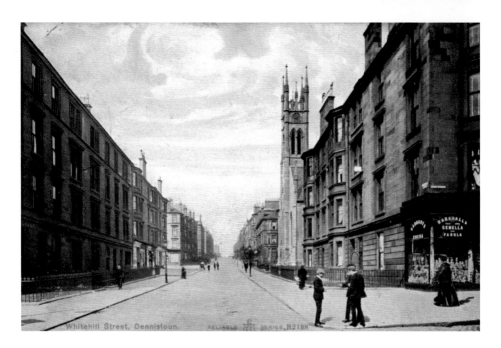

Whitehill Street

Whitehill Street is an example of many Dennistoun streets that have survived the ravages of the developers. Comparing these two images more than 100 years apart shows little change, except for the road signs and volume of traffic. Laid out from the mid-nineteenth century, the street takes its name from the Whitehall estate on which part of the suburb was built. Dennistoun was named after the entrepreneur Alexander dennistnoun, who owned most of the land. The church in the images was one of the earliest constructions. It was built for a United Presbyterian congregation in 1869/70 and is still used as a place of worship.

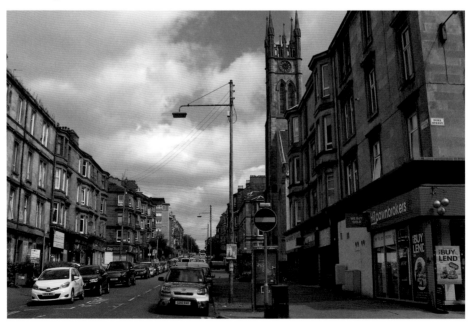

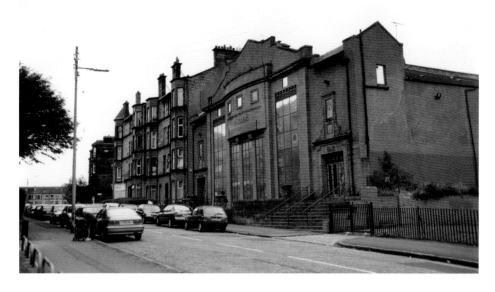

Dennistoun Parade Cinema

Seen above shortly before its demolition in 1921, Dennistoun Parade cinema in Meadowpark Street, Dennistoun. It closed after forty years, but reopened again as a private cinema from 1969 to 1986 as the New Parade. After stints as both a bingo hall and bar, it finally closed its doors around 2007. In comparison, the Riddrie Vogue has survived as bingo hall, and is a wonderful example of the Art Deco picture palaces that once graced the city. Built in 1938, and facing onto Cumbernauld Road, it is one of the remaining, recognisable relics of that bygone era of film fanaticism, which, in its heyday, entranced the population of Glasgow.

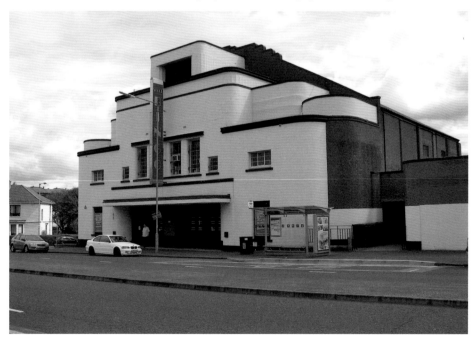

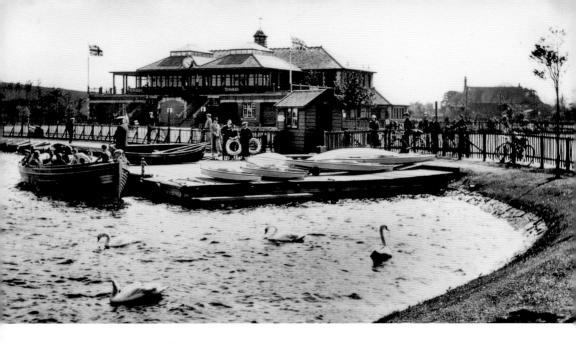

Hogganfield and Franfield Lochs

Glasgow grew on the banks of the Molendinar Burn, which has its source at Hogganfield Loch. Hogganfield and Frankfield Lochs were purchased by the city in 1667 to ensure a water supply to the town and power the mills. It has retained the rights to the water supply ever since. Hogganfield was deepened, and an island created when it was being developed into a park in the 1920s. The island became a bird sanctuary and, in 1998, the loch was ascribed the status of a Local Nature Reserve. It now provides a habitat for migrating and wintering water-fowl. The 1930s tearoom and boathouse no longer exist.

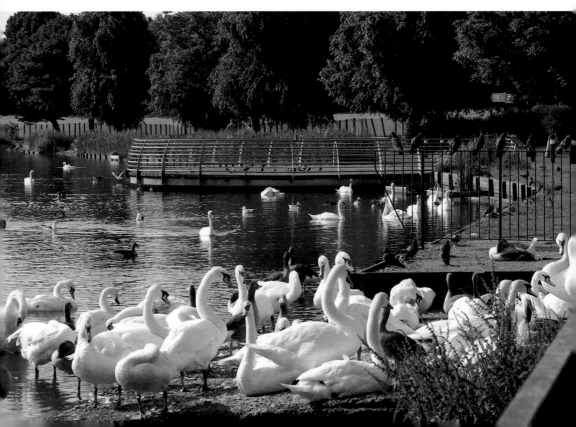

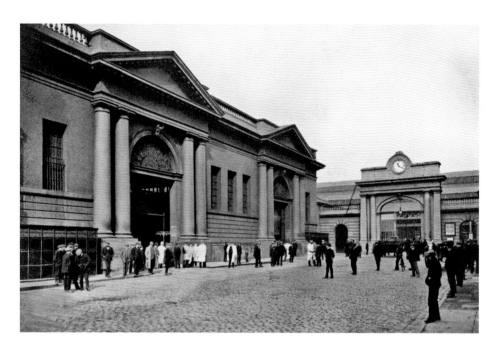

Graham Square

Graham Square was a failed eighteenth-century speculative venture by James Graham, owner of the Saracen Head Inn. The adjacent land was later acquired by Glasgow in 1818 for its cattle and horse market. The square became the venue for the annual feeing day, when farmers and workers negotiated contracts for the following year. Seen here in 1914 and 2014, the predominant feature remains the later Roman Doric market entrances to the west and north of the Square. The markets have entirely gone, and the western façade has been preserved by the unusual method of propping it against the new housing built behind it.

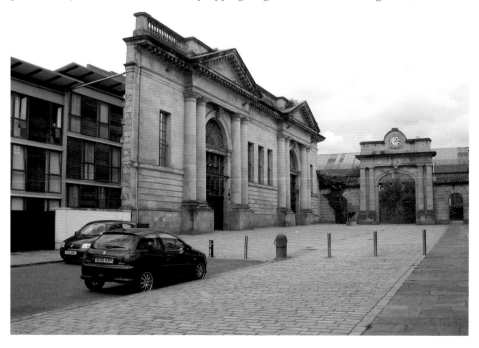

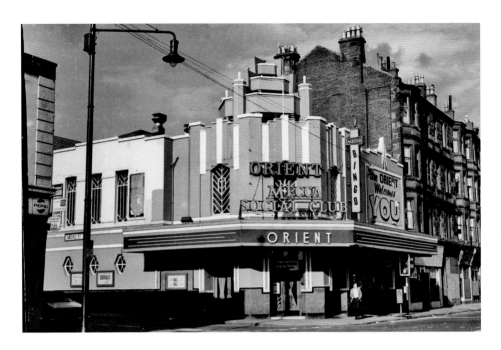

Orient Bingo Hall

Looking more like a wedding cake, in its vivid pink glory in 1974, is the Orient Bingo Hall on the Gallowgate. This early 1930s picture house at Sword Street is another of the many cinemas that could be found throughout the East End, each with an exotic name to entice their audience into glorious and (hopefully) luxurious settings. It could seat a remarkable 2,570 patrons in its huge hall. That it could anticipate such numbers in the face of many competitors is indicative of the density of the local population during this period. New housing has replaced the one-time location of this picture palace.

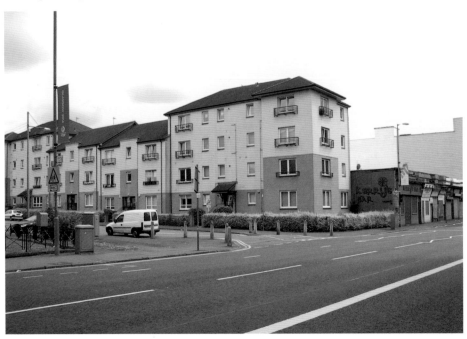

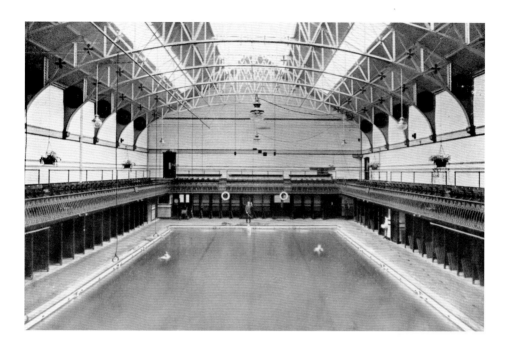

Whitevale Street Public Baths

The large (men's) swimming pool at the Glasgow Corporation's Whitevale Street public baths, as seen in 1914. Opened in 1902, this provision had separate pools for men and woman, along with a 'steamie'. It also had a seemingly unique facility for Glasgow at the time – a Turkish bath. The Whitevale Street entrance to the baths still clings to life, but now leads nowhere, the large pool building having been demolished in 2012. The 2014 photograph repeats an increasingly iconic image of the old baths, with the brutalist architecture of the 1960s Bluevale flats in the background.

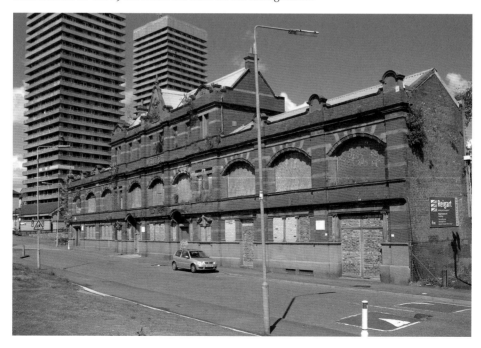

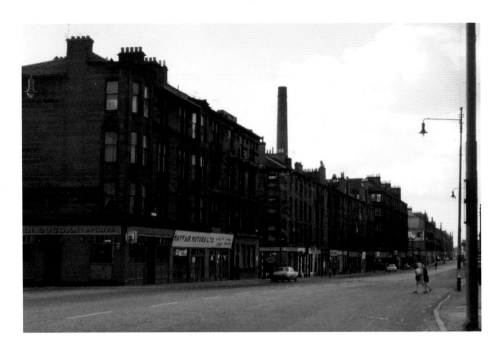

Gallowgate Tenements

During the late 1970s, these tenements on the Gallowgate from Tylefield Street to Abercomby Street were demolished. Orr Street, Wesleyan Street, Cubie Street, Soho Street, Tylefield Street and Rowchester Street, all leading off the Gallowgate into Mile End, were completely eliminated and the vacated ground was used to lay out the extensive Crownpoint Sports Centre. Crownpoint was an eighteenth-century estate in eastern Mile End, the mansion house of which was demolished during the same period as the tenements. Seen below is a sports day being held at the Centre on 14 June 2014.

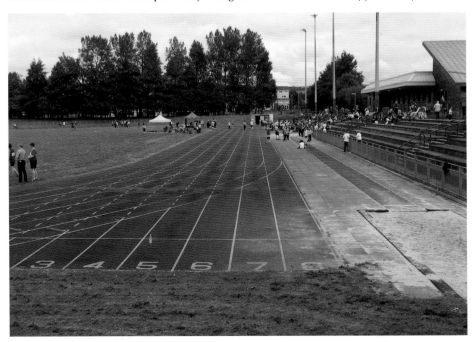

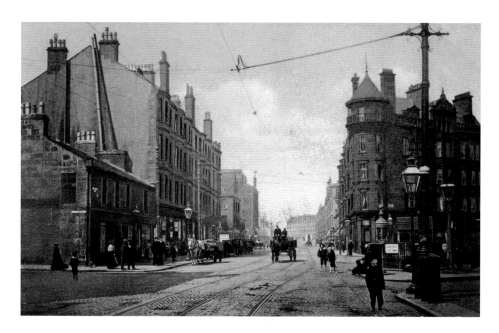

Looking West Along the Gallowgate Through Parkhead Cross, *c.* 1905
Parkhead originated in the mid-eighteenth century at the junction of several very old roads as a community of weavers and miners. Many of their dwellings were of the two-storey variety as seen above at Burgher Street. During the development of Parkhead Cross in the Edwardian era, this particular building was replaced by an ornate five-storey edifice, which was occupied by the Savings Bank of Glasgow. The new building and the adjacent tenement remain the only white sandstone structures in an otherwise uniform collection of imposing red sandstone cliffs, built to enhance the prestige of the Cross.

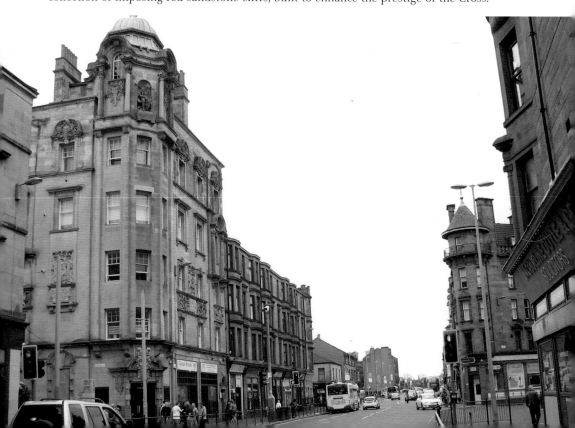

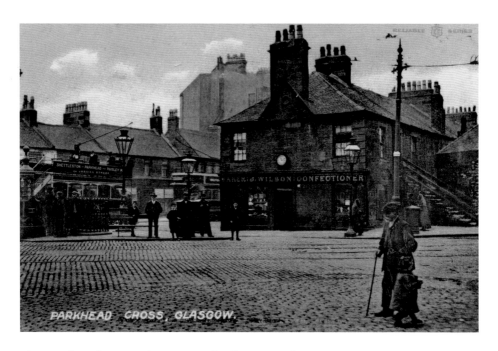

The Junction of Westmuir Street and Tollcross Road, *c.* 1900
The two-storey building housed local baker J. Wilson's, with a post office on the upper floor accessed by external stairs. It was one of the first substantial buildings at the crossroads that became Parkhead Cross. These locations seem to attract people who wish to socialise or simply watch the world go by – they did in 1900 and do so now. In 1905, the old building was replaced by another addition to the array of elaborate tenements now found at the Cross.

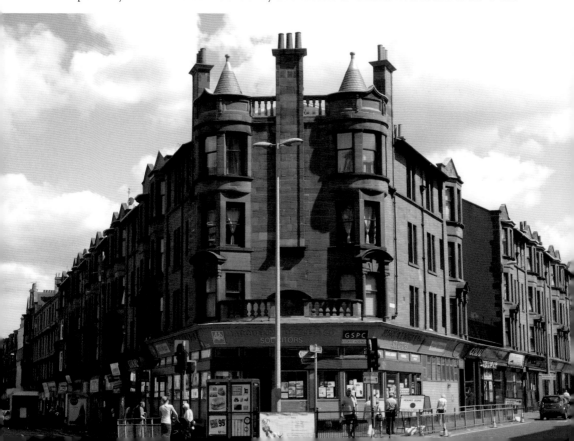

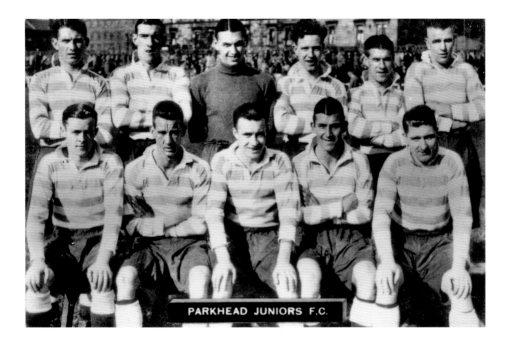

PARKHEAD JUNIORS F.C.

Parkhead

The history of Parkhead is dominated by Beardmore's huge Parkhead Forge and football. Shown above in their own hooped football jerseys, Parkhead Juniors reflect the district's close association with Celtic FC. Founded in 1880, before Celtic, the team played at various local grounds. Although Glasgow has a tradition of athletic success, there is still little doubt that football predominates as the sport to pursue, inculcated since earliest childhood. That there are alternatives has been emphasised recently with the Commonwealth Games sited on Parkhead's doorstep. Below, some of the Guyana cycling team are caught at traffic lights at Parkhead Cross as they explore the routes of the cycling events.

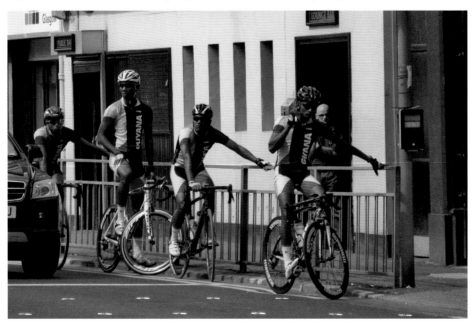

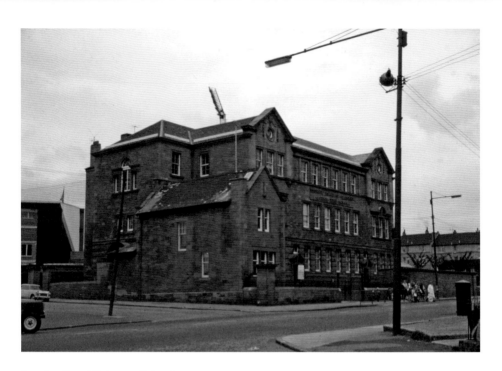

London Road Primary School

London Road Primary School in 1974, with the infants being assisted by a traditional lollipop man. At the present time, several of the older red sandstone primary schools in the East End appear to be under threat of demolition, with this 1907 school being removed in 2014 as part of Celtic FC's remodelling of its entrance for the Commonwealth Games. The site is now a temporary car park while it awaits the construction of a multipurpose facility for the club. With the school's removal, the eastern Lisbon Lions Stand is now more fully exposed to view.

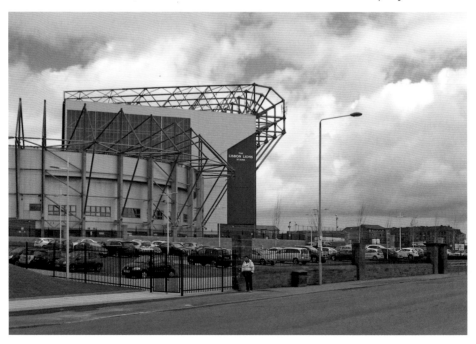

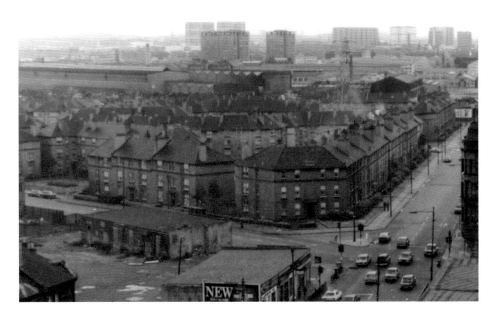

Inter-war Tenements and the Remnants of Arrol's Dalmarnock Works
View from the Helenvale Flats, 1974. The central area was levelled to provide a site for the construction of the Emirates Arena and the Chris Hoy Velodrome, both venues for events in the Commonwealth Games. These facilities, along with Celtic Park, provide a concentration of resources west of Springfield Road that can attract major sporting events to the city, as well as providing facilities for local people to enjoy. The old Arrol's works have disappeared beneath the new Clyde Gateway road, which provides more direct access to the area.

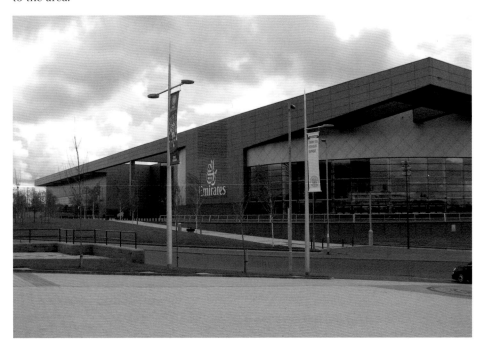

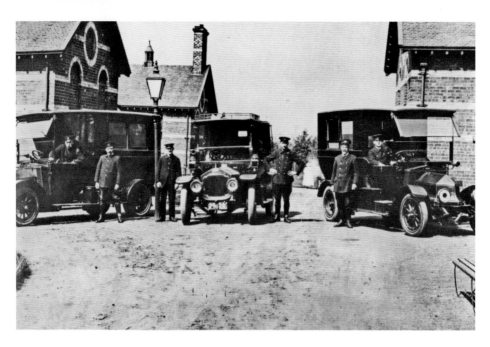

Drivers Pose with Ambulances in Belvidere Hospital Just Before the First World War
Belvidere was closed in 1990 and demolished with no attempt to preserve an example of its innovative pavilions and only a half-hearted endeavour to safeguard the doctors' building (now a ruin). It was built as a Fever Hospital for Glasgow, while Lightburn Hospital in Carntyne, pictured below, was a joint venture of 1896 with Lanarkshire for the same purpose. The original buildings at Lightburn were eventually replaced and, after recently avoiding closure, the four-ward hospital continues to provide a variety of services to the older members of the East End community.

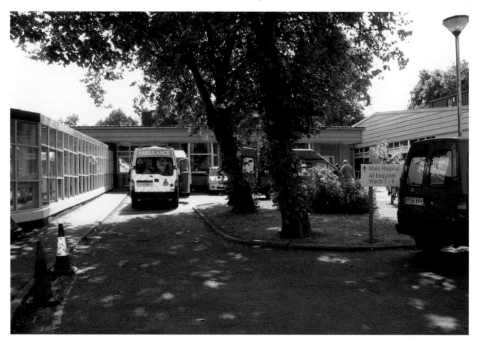

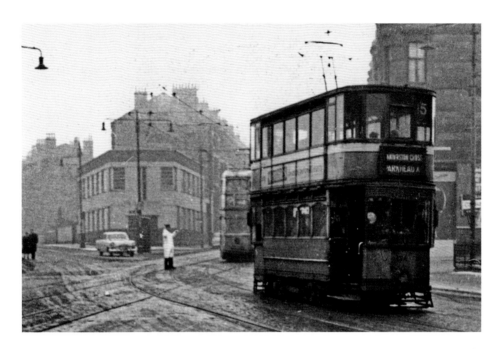

'You're Having a Giraffe?' The gable end at the junction of Old Shettleston Road and Shettleston Road

Gable end painting gained a new popularity in the lead up to the Commonwealth Games, with numerous examples being displayed throughout the city. The old derelict Glasgow Corporation lamp lighting works, seen to the left of the tram, were demolished in 2013. The entry to Shettleston from Parkhead was livened up by a new artwork the following year courtesy of Shettleston Housing Association, students at Eastbank Academy and the arts company Art Pistol.

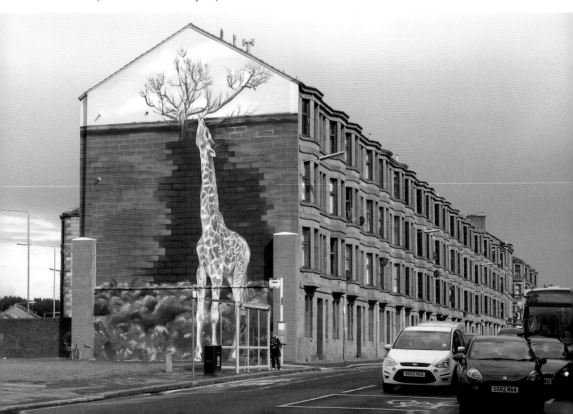

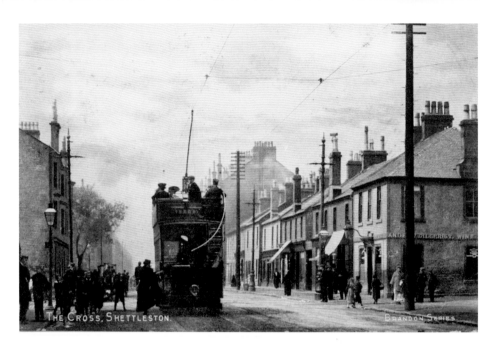

Shettleston Cross, Sited at the Junction of Shettleston Road and Welshott Road
The district's name has nothing to do with the weaving industry in the earlier village, a view that arose from a designation of 'shuttleston' being used around the eighteenth century. It is far more ancient. As early as 1179, the locale was referred to by the Bishop of Glasgow as the residence of Sedin's son or daughter, and then as Schedinestun. It was from this that the present name evolved. Shettleston was incorporated into Glasgow in 1912, with Main Street becoming Shettleston Road.

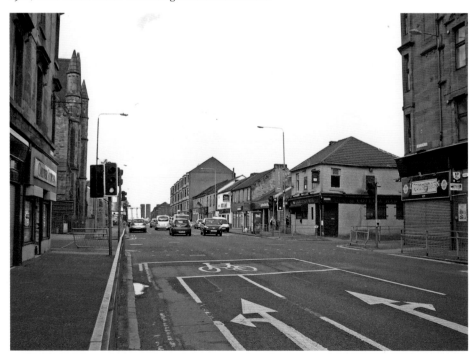

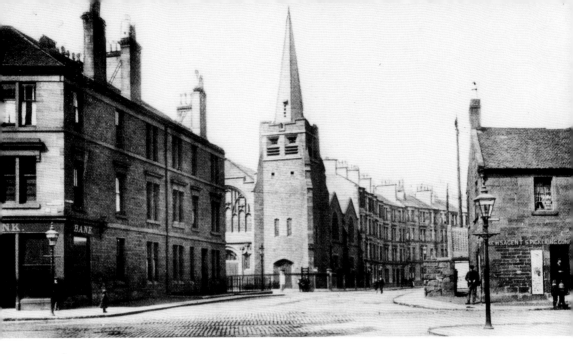

Station Road

In about 1900, Station Road, in the Middlequarter of Shettleston still led to Shettleston station. Subsequently renamed Annick Street after incorporation into Glasgow, this route has been curtailed by supermarket development, and is now something of a backwater. The only significant feature remaining is Shettleston New Church of Scotland. Its recent history saw it change from Eastbank church to its present designation in 2007 with the closure of Carntyne Old Church. Built from 1901–04 for a United Presbyterian congregation, the church has an outstanding dark wood interior in the Glasgow Style that is worth seeing.

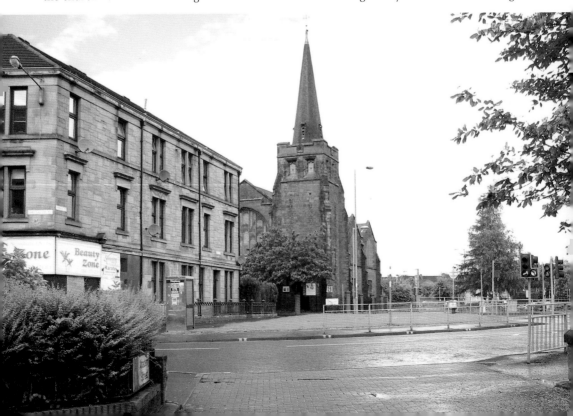

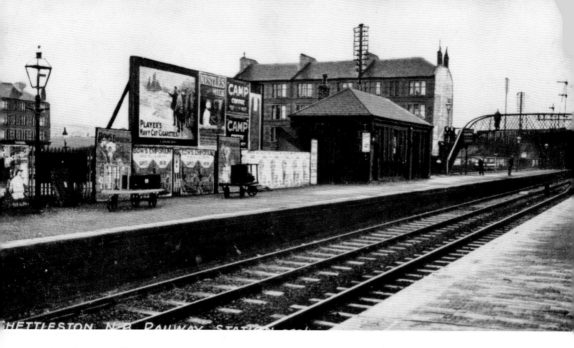

SHETTLESTON N.B. RAILWAY STATION

Shettleston Railway Station

Shettleston railway station was opened during the expansion of the railway companies in late Victorian times. This was a response to the community's own rapid increases in population, commerce and industry, due to its proximity to Glasgow. With such growth there came the increased demand for the transportation of goods and workforce, in the days prior to the introduction of the trams. Some of those who could afford to also took the opportunity to move from the city to the suburban villas that were being built close to the stations, choosing to commute to their jobs in the city.

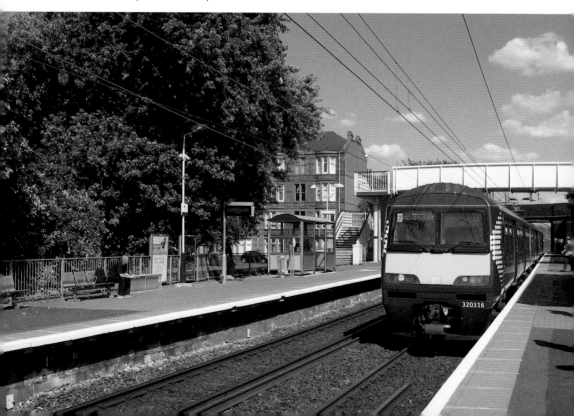

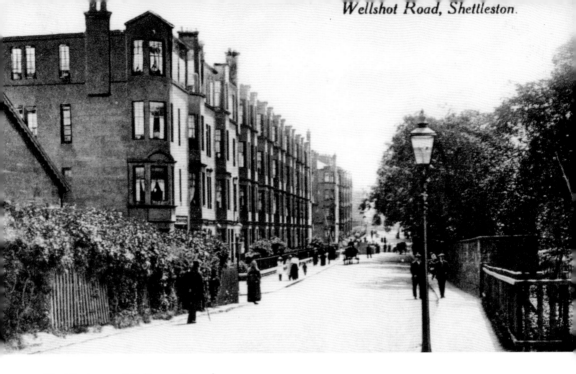

Shettleston and Tollcross Boundary

The boundary between Shettleston and Tollcross was traditionally taken to be the Tollcross Burn. Running westwards, it enters Tollcross Park at Wellshot Road, before turning south to eventually enter the Clyde at Dalbeth. Wellshot Road was the main route between the two communities. Seen here looking towards Tollcross from the Shettleston side of the Burn, the road crosses a bridge in the far distance, under which the culverted stream enters the park. It flows through the old estate in the open air until passing beneath Tollcross Road, and can only truly be seen again in its natural state once it enters St Peter's Cemetery.

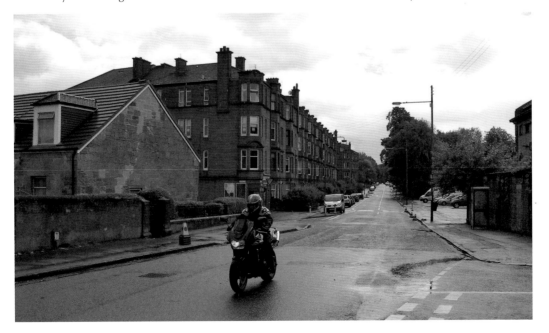

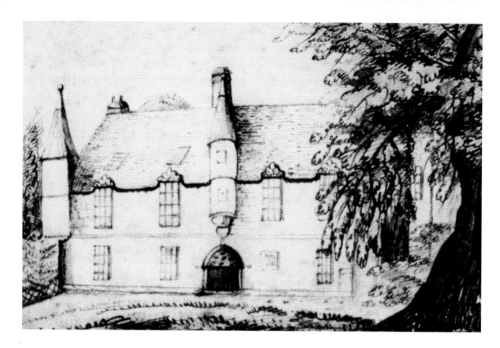

Tollcross House

This sketch of Tollcross House depicts the residence that was replaced by the present mansion shown below. This earlier building was most probably built by the previous owners of Tollcross, the Corbet family, who had been in the area from at least 1580. The property was acquired by the Dunlops in 1810 and the impressive family house was built in 1846. The remnant of the once extensive estate was purchased in 1896 by Glasgow Corporation to provide another park. For a time, the mansion housed a children's museum, but it now provides residential accommodation for older people.

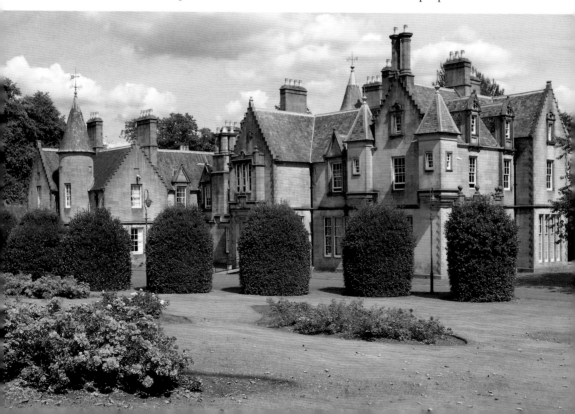

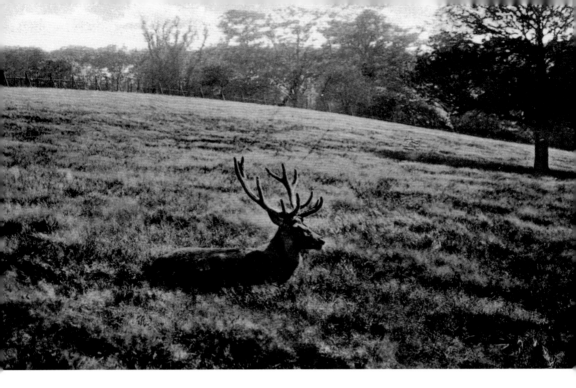

Tollcross Estate

Prior to its purchase by the city, the Tollcross estate included a deer park that fronted onto Tollcross Road. This gave its name to Deerpark Gardens on the opposite side of the road. The deer have gone, and the land once occupied by them is now used for the International Rose Trial Garden. The park continues to accommodate a number of grazing animals, which, at times, include Highland cattle and a variety of sheep. It also has a children's city farm, which is located in the courtyard of the old coach house off Wellshot Road.

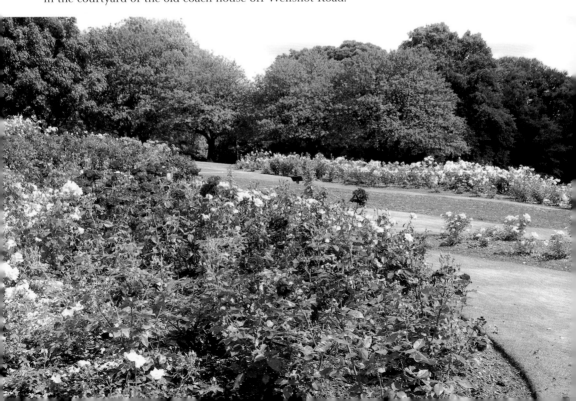

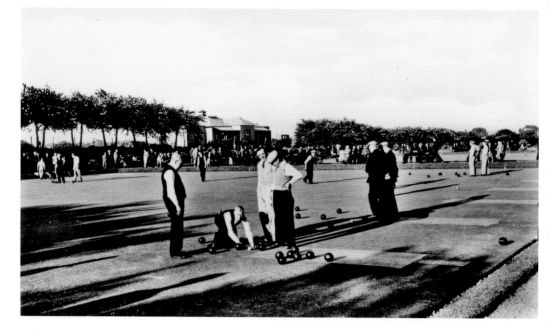

Tollcross Park

The recreational spaces of Glasgow's parks have always been responsive to changes in the public's interests. This is particularly notable in the construction of the sports complex in Tollcross Park in 1996 – a project not without its objectors. Bowling was played on the lawns of Tollcross Mansion while it was still a private property, and was a regular feature in the park for many years, but it has now been discontinued. Another innovation, on Shettleston Hill within the park, is the current home of the Glasgow Baseball Association's two teams – Glasgow Comets and Glasgow Galaxy. Seen here is Glasgow Galaxy *v*. the Aberdeen Oilers in April 2014.

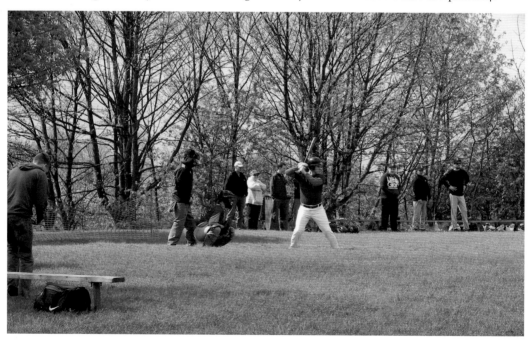

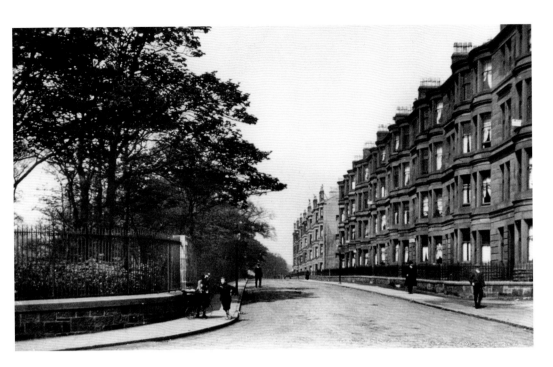

Wellshot Road from Tollcross Road *c.* 1906, with an Entrance to Tollcross Park to the Left
The entrance to the park was remodelled in 2005 with metalwork designed by sculptor Andy Scott depicting elements from the 'Who Killed Cock Robin' nursery rhyme – closely associated in recent years with Tollcross. Through the trees, the sports centre built in 1996 can just be glimpsed. It was a venue for the swimming events in the 2014 Commonwealth Games. The gap seen in the tenements in the 1906 photograph was the site of Green's Cinema, opened in 1910, the district's only picture house.

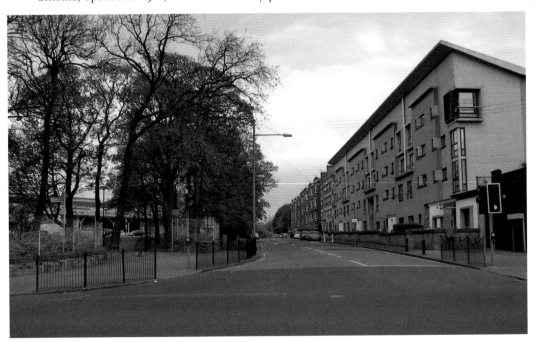

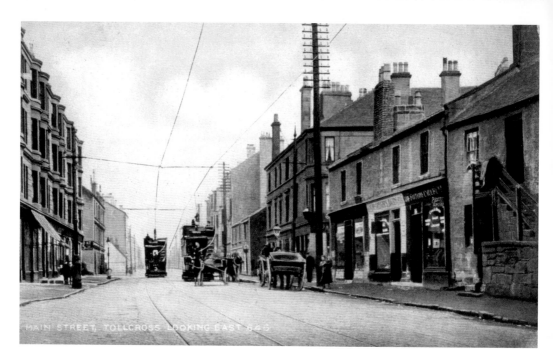

Main Street

Main Street in Tollcross was changed to Tollcross Road in 1912 when the community was annexed to Glasgow. This was to avoid confusion with the Main Street in Bridgeton. The *c.* 1906 image shows the junction with Wellshot Road, which was reputedly the site of an actual cross or crossroads where toll, or tax, would be levied on the passage of goods. This in turn gave its name to the area. A good deal of nineteenth-century architecture can still be seen on Tollcross Road, but those houses to the right were removed to open up access to Braidfauld Street.

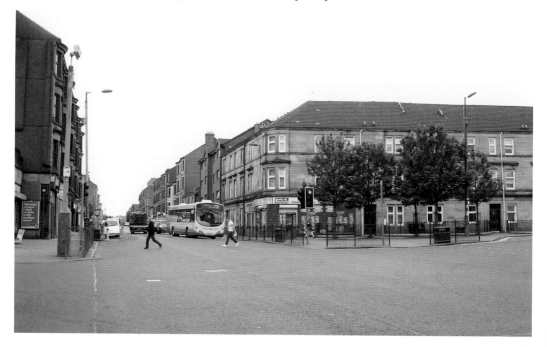

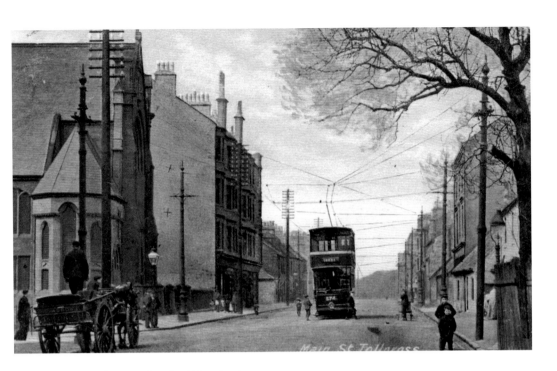

Victoria Tollcross Church of Scotland

The front of the red sandstone Victoria Tollcross Church of Scotland can be seen here in both images. With the demolition of the iconic Tollcross Central Church a few years after a fire in 1990, this is now the oldest congregation in the community, its first church being built in 1867. The church faces onto Tollcross Road, where the only hazard in 1906 appears to have been the occasional tram and horse-drawn cart. Modern Tollcross Road has become a very busy thoroughfare, where cars now park on the pavements rather than having pedestrians walking in the road.

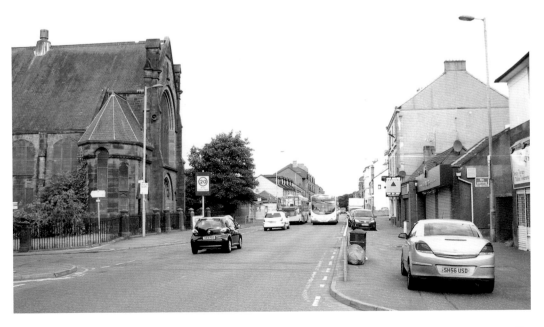

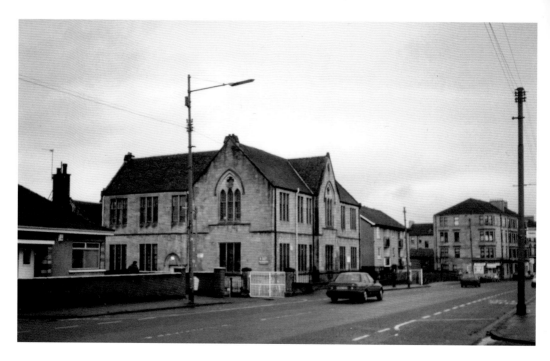

Tollcross Public School at the Junction of Tollcross Road and Fullarton Avenue, *c.* 1975
There is reported to have been a school in Tollcross as early as 1786, but education remained largely a matter to be dealt with by religious authorities rather than anyone else prior to the Education (Scotland) Act of 1872. This act made basic education compulsory and established school boards to implement this legislation. Tollcross Public School was built in response to this act and served the community until 1975. In 2012, the site was cleared to facilitate the construction of a supported accommodation facility by Loretto Care.

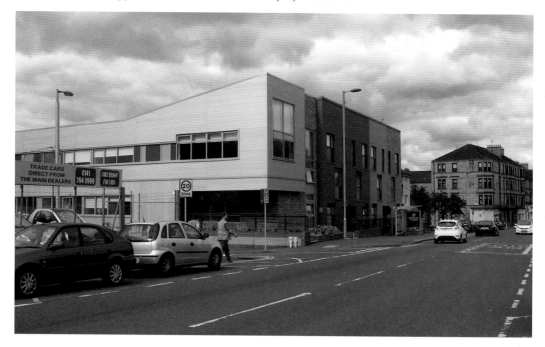

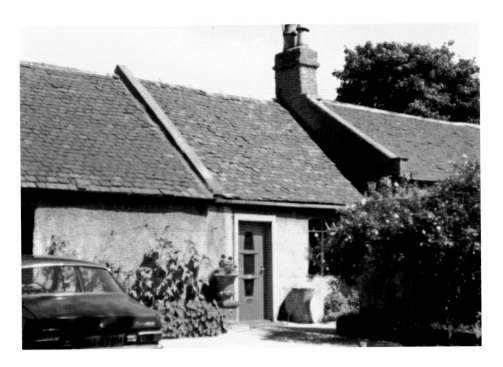

Egypt Farm

Where but in the East End would you find both Egypt and the pyramids? The one-time fields and orchards attaching to Egypt Farm off Dalness Street, Tollcross, now produce a crop of houses, with only the farm buildings surviving at its core. The origin of the name is much speculated upon, but remains a mystery. The prime candidate is a returning soldier from the Napoleonic Wars who purchased the farm and renamed it in commemoration of his experiences. With an Egypt, one needs pyramids, and these have been supplied courtesy of the Forge shopping centre at Parkhead.

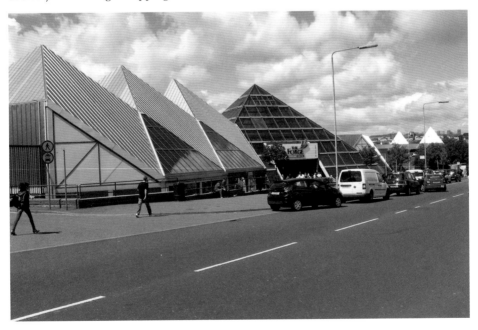

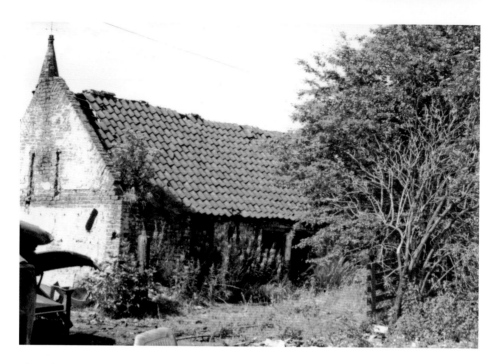

The Oldest House in Tollcross

The oldest house in Tollcross, photographed here in 1975, with the newest on its site at Corbett Place. Probably dating from the late eighteenth or early nineteenth century, the building was of the simplest construction and had no plumbing for running water. This may have been obtained from the nearby Battle Burn. There were no electrical fittings, but each room had a small cast-iron fireplace. A byre was attached for the animals. The roof was of pantiles, a very distinctive feature much used in early Calton. The People's Palace had hoped save it as a weaver's cottage, but was unsuccessful.

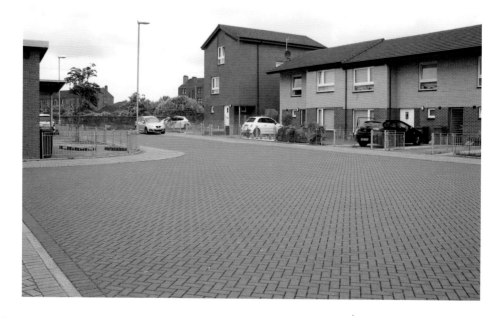

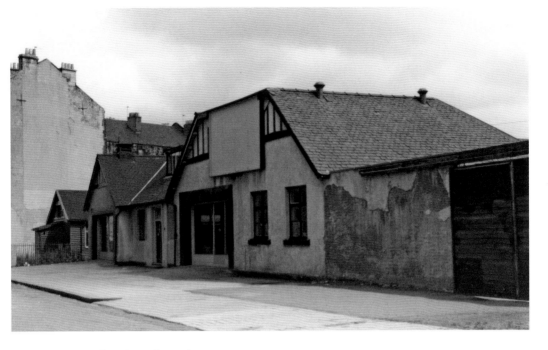

The Miners' Institute in Corbett Street, 1975

This was a one-time resource for the community of miners living in Tollcross. With the establishment of the National Fire Service in 1941, the institute became Corbett Street Fire Station. It remained in use until Parkhead station opened in 1952 and took over its responsibilities. In more recent years it was used as a car showroom. Along with the adjacent Salvation Army hall, the old buildings were taken down. The site is now mostly occupied by Haydale Care Home, one of a number of private homes to spring up in the Tollcross area.

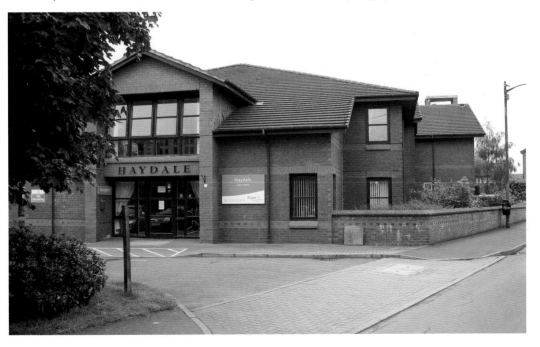

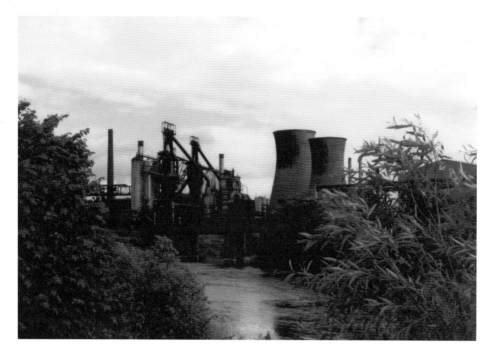

Clyde Ironworks and the M74 Road Bridge Spanning the River Clyde
The cooling towers of Clyde Iron Works at Carmyle dominated the local skyline, and the furnaces lit up the night for centuries before the works closed. This view upriver on the Clyde from Easterhill was captured in 1975. For decades, Easterhill was covered in the waste products of the plant until restored recently by Clyde Gateway for development purposes. The ironworks view has been replaced by the new road bridge at Auchenshuggle for the M74 extension. Its support girders spanned the Clyde on 14 June 2010.

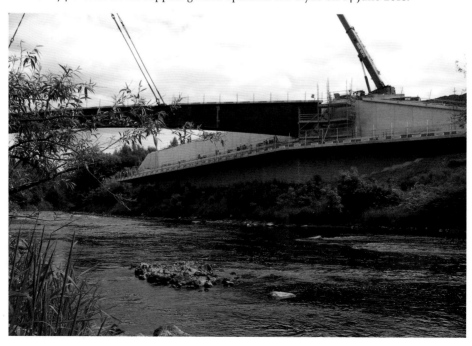

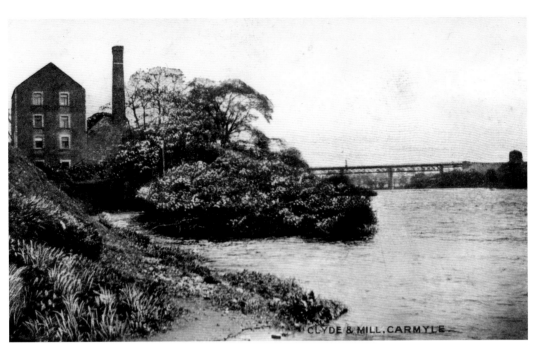

The Mill at Carmyle on the Clyde, c. 1905, Looking Upriver

There had been a mill on the Clyde at Carmyle since at least 1268, when the Bishop of Glasgow, John Cheyam, instructed one to be built on the church lands to grind flour and meal. Production at the site continued for more than 600 years thereafter, into the beginning of the twentieth century, but in private hands by that time. When milling ended, the buildings were used as a sawdust mill in the 1920s, and ultimately a rag store. Although now gone, there is significant industrial archaeology still in evidence around the riverside.

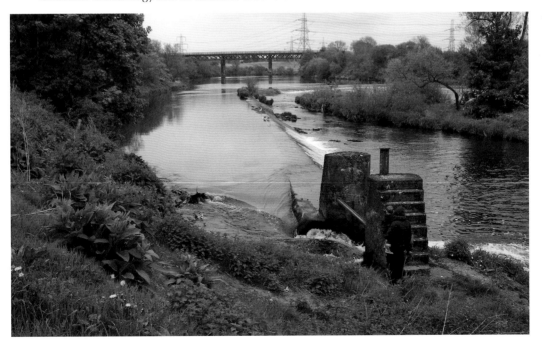

Select Bibliography

Adams, Gordon, *A History of Bridgeton & Dalmarnock* (Glasgow, Hill & Hay Ltd, 1990)
Adams, Gordon, *A History of Tollcross & Dalbeth* (Glasgow, Clydeside Press, 1992)
Adams, Gordon *Glasgow East* (The History Press, 2007)
Corporation of Glasgow, *Municipal Glasgow; Its Evolution and Enterprises* (Glasgow, Anderson Ross, 1914)
Fisher, Joe, *The Glasgow Encyclopaedia (*Edinburgh, Mainstream Publishing, 1994)
Louden, T., *The Cinemas of Cinema City* (1983)
Williamson, Elizabeth *et al, The Buildings of Scotland Glasgow* (Penguin Books, 1990)
Wilson, Margaret, *Carmyle Reminiscences* (Glasgow, Carmyle Reminiscence Group, 1992)

See also www.eastglasgowhistory.com

Image Sources

The following images are reproduced by the consent of the owners.

Upper Images:
   Adams, Gordon – pages 27, 28, 39, 44–47, 49, 50, 52–58, 68, 71, 73, 91–95
   Clyde Gateway – page 51
Lower Images:
   Adams, Gordon – All images except the following;
      Blaikie, Gerry – pages 64
      Clyde Gateway – pages 51–56

My apologies to any copyright holders that I was unaware of and have therefore been not included attribution.